D1375026

CAR

'The purpose of this book is show you how to acquire the 'psychological 'muscle' to cope with the vicissitudes of life in such a way that virtually nothing can floor you. No, we're not aiming to make you insensitive, or to kid you that pain doesn't exist. In all probability you will, from time to time, continue to experience disappointments and frustrations, and suffer the pain of grief, sadness and sorrow as everyone else. The world is certainly no rose garden.

What we do maintain, is that with the right mental attitude you can take most of the sting out of pain, when occasionally some personal misfortune knocks you off your perch, or life gives you a rough time.

We intend to help you develop a way of thinking about yourself and the world around you that, if you work at it, will enable you to cope more effectively with your life when the going gets tougher than you would have thought possible.'

Windy Dryden & Jack Gordon

Also in
Orient Paperbacks

How to cope
When the
going
gets tough

Windy Dryden & Jack Gordon

Orient
Paperbacks
DELHI | MUMBAI | HYDERABAD

LONDON BOROUGH OF SUTTON LIBRARY SERVICE (WAL)	
02458498	
Askews	Oct-2007
158.1	

www.orientpaperbacks.com

ISBN 81-222-0350-7

1st Published in Orient Paperbacks 2004
2nd Printing 2005

How to Cope When the Going Gets Tough

© Windy Dryden and Jack Gordon 1994

Published in arrangement with
Sheldon Press, England

Cover design by Vision Studio

Published by
Orient Paperbacks
(A division of Vision Books Pvt. Ltd.)
Madarsa Road, Kashmere Gate, Delhi-110 006

Printed in India at
Jay Kay Offset Printers, Delhi-110 041

Cover Printed at
Ravindra Printing Press, Delhi-110 006

Contents

ONE

When the Going Gets Tough, Become Tough-minded

*W*e aim to help you reach a level of psychological fitness or inner strength, whereby you will feel comfortable, and not overwhelmed, when life presents you with tough choices.

The objective is to show how to acquire the 'psychological muscle' to cope with the vicissitudes of life in such a way that virtually nothing can floor you.

How to Cope When the Going Gets Tough gives you a clear explanation of a sound and effective means of acquiring true mental health and happiness. This method will help you to develop the psychological strength and stamina you need, to cope successfully with the stresses and challenges of everyday living in this increasingly irrational world.

Although we are primarily concerned here with helping you to develop psychological strength and fitness, a few remarks on the related subject of physical health and fitness will not be out of place, and will help set the scene for what is to follow.

Imagine you are preparing yourself for a long journey over difficult terrain. Some of it is mountainous and you may have to negotiate river crossings and various other hazards may confront you. In addition to providing yourself with a good map and the right equipment, what else might you do in advance to improve your chances of successfully reaching your destination?

Even if you are reasonably fit and healthy, you would be wise to ensure that you possess sufficient muscle strength and stamina to carry you through those parts of your journey that could impose severe demands on you. Also, there is that all-important pump inside you—your heart. How much extra effort can your heart supply in an emergency, or when the going gets tough?

Since this is not a manual on attaining physical fitness, we need say no more except to add that if you really want to develop psychological strength and endurance, to see you through life with a minimum of wear and tear on your nervous system, a reasonable degree of physical fitness will certainly not go amiss.

You need to be fit enough to meet the demands of your chosen lifestyle, and to have that little bit in reserve to enable you to spend the occasional night in a disco or nightclub, or play an extra round of golf or a set of tennis game without feeling exhausted. We think the old Roman maxim 'a healthy mind in a healthy body' represents a sensible and attainable ideal. The two don't necessarily go together, but if they do, you've got a worthwhile bonus.

OK, enough on physical fitness. Now let's get down to seeing how you can go about developing real mental health and emotional muscle, to enable you to surmount the difficulties and challenges of everyday life and attain your chosen goals in life.

What it Means to be Tough Minded

When life is going smoothly and everything you want is coming your way, it's easy to lull yourself into a false sense of security. When skies are blue and the sun is shining, it is easy to imagine that trouble is something that happens to somebody else. Often, you cannot imagine anything going seriously wrong, or any problem arising that you cannot comfortably deal with.

Of course, life does have its spells when everything looks rosy and seemingly set to stay that way. Unfortunately, it is often when we are feeling most complacent that things go suddenly and drastically wrong. To take an example, let's say you have been doing well in your job, and one day your boss calls you into his office. Normally you are due for a salary increase about this time, so in you go, a smile of anticipation already on your lips. Your boss hands you a slip of paper: it's your redundancy notice. You can scarcely believe your eyes. What? Me made redundant? Or to give another example, you return home one night and discover that your house has been burgled, and that everything of value has been taken.

This type of occurrence — and many worse ones— are happening all the time. So how would you react if confronted with a personal shock or tragedy? Are you sufficiently confident of your psychological strength and ability, to withstand the shock and stress of a severe personal loss, and to motivate yourself to take some kind of constructive action to mitigate the worst effects of your predicament? Or would you experience the emotional "wobblies", and feel so upset that you would feel helpless to do anything at all about it?

The whole point of this book is to show you how to acquire the psychological 'muscle' to cope with the vicissitudes of life in such a way that virtually nothing can floor you. No, we're not aiming to make you insensitive, or to kid you that pain doesn't exist. In all probability you'll still suffer from time to time the pain of grief, sadness, or sorrow, and experience the same disappointments and frustrations as everyone else. The world is certainly no rose garden. What we do maintain, though, is that with the right mental attitude you can take most of the sting out of pain, when occasionally some personal misfortune knocks you off your perch, or life gives you a rough time.

We aim to help you reach a level of psychological fitness or inner strength whereby you will feel uncomfortable, rather than overwhelmed, when life presents you with tough choices. When you reach that stage, you will find you can make optimum use of your natural problem-solving abilities, to recover from negative experiences — and sometimes, you can even put such experiences to your advantage.

You Feel as You Think!

We are going to teach you a way of thinking about yourself and the world around you that, if you work at it and practise it, will enable you to cope more effectively with your life when the going gets tougher than you would have thought possible. The credit for this important breakthrough belongs to Dr Albert Ellis, a famous clinical psychologist in the United States. It is known as Rational Emotive Behaviour Therapy, or REBT for short, and many practitioners throughout the world have used, and are continuing to use (with impressive results), this well-tested innovative system to reduce or eliminate common emotional problems.

'You feel as you think' stands for an important REBT Insight, which we shall call REBT Insight No. 1

REBT Insight No. 1. You feel as you think and all your thoughts, feelings, and behaviour are interrelated.

Many studies over the past few years have shown that human emotions do not magically exist in their own right, but almost always stem directly from ideas, beliefs, or attitudes, and can usually be changed by modifying one's thinking processes. In other words, if you change the way you think, you also tend to change the way you feel, and the way you subsequently act or behave. If feelings stem directly from our attitudes or beliefs, it follows that common emotional problems like anxiety, guilt, depression, and anger stem not from what happens to us, but from our attitudes about what happens to us. So it would seem that the way to change disturbed feelings would be to modify the thinking processes by which we create them. That is the meaning of 'you feel as you think'.

Can We Change How We Think?

We can anticipate a question that may well have occurred to you. 'You say that we can change how we feel by changing the way we think, and we use the words "modify one's thinking processes". What precisely do you mean by that? Are you implying that we need to make some kind of specific change in our thinking in order to change disturbed feelings and behaviour?' Our answer to that question is, 'Yes, your question goes right to the core of the way in which feelings are created, and can be changed, by examining the specific thoughts or attitudes that people have about the things that happen to them and that they mistakenly consider to be the cause of their emotional problems.'

However, this is not to imply that other people's behaviour towards us is unimportant. For example, losing your job or the break-up of an important relationship does matter. These events contribute towards what we feel, but do not by themselves cause our feelings. This is really good news, because if losing one's jobs or the break-up of one's relationship always caused us to feel terribly upset, then everybody who was ever sacked, made redundant, or broke up with someone in a close relationship would feel overwhelmed — and we know that this is not so. The key question here, as hinted above, is which kind of attitudes or thoughts create the emotional turmoil and which kind do not. Let us now address that question before we proceed further.

Developing 'Tough-minded' Thinking

We distinguish two kinds of thinking here: 'rational or tough-minded' thinking and 'irrational or crumble-minded' thinking. Each of these two kinds of thinking leads to specific kinds of emotional response.

Rational or tough-minded attitudes will lead to healthy negative feelings — such as annoyance, sadness, or disappointment — about negative events such as being rejected or made redundant. We call these attitudes 'constructive', because they help us to cope with these negative events and can motivate us to do something to improve our situation.

Conversely, irrational or crumble-minded beliefs or attitudes will lead to unhealthy negative feelings such as anger, hurt, or self-pity about the same negative events. We call these attitudes 'unconstructive', because they neither help us to cope effectively with our misfortune, nor motivate us to improve our circumstances — in fact, they may even lead us into actions that make things worse for us. For example, anger may lead to violence with unpredictable consequences. Anger is quite different from annoyance, and it is important to be aware of the difference. When we are annoyed, we are saying in effect, 'I don't like your behaviour or the way you have treated me, but I don't hate you'. When we are angry, though, we hate the person as well as that person's behaviour. Anger and annoyance stem from quite different kinds of thinking, as we will see in a moment.

Rational vs Irrational Thinking

So far, we have introduced the concepts of healthy negative feelings and unhealthy negative feelings. We agree that healthy-negative feelings generate behaviour likely to help one to cope with one's difficulties, while unhealthy negative feelings lead to behaviour that tends to be ineffective and self-defeating.

We will now show you how to distinguish rational or tough-minded thinking from irrational or crumble-minded beliefs and attitudes.

Goals, Purposes, and Rationality. All of us have preferences and desires and we seem to be happiest when we set life goals and purposes in order to achieve these preferences. As long as we succeed in getting what we want, we usually feel happy and contented; but when we are prevented from fulfilling our desires, we experience negative emotions. Whether these emotions are healthy or unhealthy, depends upon the way we view things when our desires are not met.

REBT defines our attitudes or beliefs as rational, our feelings as healthy, and our behaviour as functional (efficient, not self-defeating) if these attitudes help us to achieve our basic goals in life. However, if our attitudes, feelings, and behaviour undermine the pursuit of our basic goals, they are deemed irrational, unhealthy, and self-defeating. Both rational and irrational philosophies can be identified and distinguished by four main characteristics, as shown in Table 1.

Table 1: Distinguishing Rational and Irrational Thinking

Rational Thinking	Irrational Thinking
✔ Consists of wants, wishes, and preferences	✗ Consists of unqualified demands, commands, and dictates.
✔ Is logical, and aids effective decision-making	✗ Is illogical, and fosters magical thinking.
✔ Is consistent with reality, encourages us to deal with things as they are, and to attempt to change them if they can be changed.	✗ Is inconsistent with reality, and discourages us from dealing with things as they are.
✔ Leads to healthy emotions, and aids constructive action.	✗ Leads to poor results for us emotionally and behaviourally.

The A-B-C Model of Emotional Disturbance

With the information we now have, we can go straight into a full explanation of the A-B-C model. Since understanding the model is of key importance to you if you wish to derive practical benefit from this book, we have used a typical example of a person suddenly being made redundant. This is an experience many people can relate to and will help to 'personalise' the model.

The A-B-C model is a device to help us understand how common emotional problems are not caused by unpleasant experiences. Perhaps this will become clear if you look carefully at Table 2 on page 18. First, though, you will need to know what the letters **A**, **B**, and **C** represent:

16

'A' — The Activating Event. For example, suppose you feel seriously depressed about something, such as being made redundant. In this instance, the loss of your job is the Activating Event, and is represented by Block **A** in Table 2. Generally speaking, whatever it is that you feel upset about, is called the Activating Event. Some typical 'A' events are rejection, betrayal, criticism, neglect and being deprived of what we want.

'C' — Consequences of the Activating Event. It stands for emotional and behavioural *Consequences* that are associated with the Activating Events. There are two distinct sets of Consequences in Block C: healthy negative emotions and unhealthy negative emotions. Both sets of Consequences are negative because they are associated with an event normally perceived as unhappy or unfortunate, i.e. being made redundant.

'B' — Our Belief System. Block **B** consists of evaluative thoughts and views of the world and includes our basic values and core beliefs. These evaluative cognitions can be put into two groups: those that are flexible and rational, or those that are rigid, dogmatic, and irrational.

The group of *rational beliefs* (rBs) lead directly to healthy negative emotions in Block C, while the group of *irrational beliefs* (iBs) create the unhealthy negative emotions in Block C. (The shorthand forms rBs and iBs will be used from here on.) Since it is extremely important that you understand this point, go back and carefully study Table 1 to help you see how it ties in with the A-B-C model shown in Table 2 on page 18 .

Now study Table 2, and observe how, in a tough situation, rBs help you to cope with it, whereas iBs undermine your resolve and decrease your chances of coping successfully with the problem.

A (Activating Event)	B (Belief System)

Rational Beliefs (rBs)

I lost my job through being made redundant.

1. I didn't want to lose my job and wish it had not happened, but there is no reason why it should not have happened.

2. Having no job is inconvenient, and a big disadvantage because of the hassle and hardship it may cause me. That's tough, but it isn't awful or horrible.

3. I don't like being out of work, and its a pain in the neck, but I can bear it.

4. It looks like it may be difficult to find another job soon, but if I fail, I fail! It doesn't mean that I am no good or that I am a total failure.

Irrational Beliefs (iBs)

1. I didn't want to be made redundant, and it absolutely shouldn't have happened!

2. It's awful that I've lost my job!

3. I can't bear it! I'll never get another job again!

4. I'm no good without a job. I'm a failure

C
(Consequences)

1. *Healthy negative emotions.* I feel sorrow and regret. I am frustrated and feel irritated, but I am very determined to keep looking for another job.

2. *Healthy behavioural consequences.* I can get new training, new skills and find out what the market wants.

1. *Unhealthy negative feelings.* I feel depressed and angry, and I feel worthless without a job.

2. *Unhealthy behavioural consequences.* I refuse to look for another job. There's no point! I'll only get 'no' for an answer every time I apply.

We need to re-emphasise that the kind of emotional response (i.e. 'healthy' or 'unhealthy') you make to unpleasant happenings will depend very much how you view these events. Thinking in rational or 'tough-minded' ways about your misfortunes will lead you to experience healthy negative feelings. By contrast, irrational or 'crumble-minded' thinking will lead you to experience unhealthy feelings and result in unconstructive behaviour.

Getting Rid of Irrational Thinking

Now if you want to replace your iBs with rBs, what do you need to do? The first step would be to identify the iBs you want to surrender, and then to examine their validity. In other words, you look for evidence that your iBs can be upheld. You challenge and question them until you are satisfied that they make no sense, and that you would be wise to replace them with more rational convictions.

This leads us on to the next letter in the alphabet — D. D stands for 'Disputing'. Taking the example we used in the A-B-C model, we will now proceed to outline the disputing procedure.

Disputing Irrational Beliefs (iBs). In Table 2 you can readily identify the iBs that would commonly be held by people who had suffered job redundancy and were experiencing unhealthy negative emotions. As we remarked previously, events in themselves don't upset us; instead, it is the view we take of them.

There are three criteria by which you can determine the validity of a belief:

Is it logical?

Is it realistic?

Does it help me achieve my goals?

Let's apply each of these questions to each iB in Table 2.

1. 'I didn't want to be made redundant, and it absolutely shouldn't have happened.'

Question: Is it logical?

Answer: The first part, 'I didn't want to be made redundant', states a wish or preference, but it is not logical to conclude that because you didn't want something to happen, therefore it absolutely shouldn't happen. It's like saying that because I wanted a sunny day, therefore it absolutely should not have rained.

Question: Is it realistic?

Answer: If you controlled the economy presumably you could order things to happen or not happen according to your wishes. Obviously you do not possess such a power nor does anyone else. It follows that it is inconsistent with reality to say that you absolutely should not have been made redundant when in fact you *were* made redundant. Demanding that something absolutely should not exist when it undoubtedly does exist is unrealistic thinking.

Question: Does it help me achieve my goals?

Answer: It's unlikely! When you demand that things must be the way you want them to be, or that what you dislike shouldn't exist, you stray outside the realm of reality. Consequently, you are more likely to sabotage your chances of achieving your goals.

2. 'It's awful that I've lost my job!

Question: Is it logical?

Answer: It *is* bad — meaning unfortunate, disadvantageous, or inconvenient — that you have lost your job. Does it logically follow that because losing your job is bad, therefore it is totally bad, 100 per cent bad? Obviously not. You can imagine worse things happening than being made redundant — you could find out you have lost your home as well.

Question: Is it realistic?

Answer: Not if you think about it!

Now, is it really totally bad that you have been made redundant? And is it so bad that it couldn't be worse? We have already shown that it could be worse, but even losing your home wouldn't be 100 per cent bad. You can never really get to 100 per cent badness because you can always imagine even worse things that could happen to you.

So nothing really is 100 per cent bad—only 99 per cent or so, and rarely even that. Of course, many people suffer enormous personal tragedies, but, terrible as they undoubtedly are, they are still not end-of-the-world horrors such as the planet being blown to bits by nuclear bombs or all life on earth annihilated by some cosmic catastrophe.

And finally, 'awful' as applied to your job loss really means that it is worse than it should *or must be.* But, however bad it is, it is exactly as bad as it is. Anything that exists, no matter how bad, must be exactly that bad. So, 'awful' is one of those words with surplus meaning and no connection to reality. We can identify degrees of badness, but nowhere can we put a mark on the scale and say that this is 'awful'.

Question: Does it help me achieve my goals?

Answer: No. If anything, 'awfulising' your misfortunes will tend to make you feel hopeless about being able to do anything constructive. If you've been made redundant, for example, you will feel very disinclined to try to find another job. After all, if you think your situation is hopeless, why bother?

3. *'I can't bear it! I'll never get another job again!'*

Question: Is it logical?

Answer: If you look at the first part of the statement, you're really telling yourself, 'I hate being made redundant, therefore I can't bear it.' It does not follow that because you strongly dislike something, you are somehow incapable of bearing it.

Now, take the second statement: 'I'll never get another job again!' This is saying that because you have lost something, you can never find a replacement. Only if you could prove that the job you lost was the last job the world would ever see, your statement would make logical sense.

Question: Is it realistic?

Answer: No. If you really could not bear something, then you would collapse and die if that thing happened to you. Yet, you are bearing what you maintain you can't bear? The truth is you can bear anything for as long as you are alive. The one thing we always do — i.e. bear what goes on in our lives — we dogmatically state that we can't do. How ridiculous!

'I will never find another job again!' How can you foretell the future? Since you cannot do that, your statement is unrealistic because there is no evidence to support it.

23

Question: Does it help me achieve my goals?

Answer: Hardly! Telling yourself that you can't bear losing your job is unlikely to put you in the right frame of mind to go job-hunting. For if you 'can't bear' being rejected, you are hardly likely to go out and risk it! And if you believe you will never get another job, the same argument applies: you will effectively prevent yourself from trying hard enough to get a job. Your belief that you will never get another job becomes a self-fulfilling prophecy, and you only succeed in perpetuating your problem of finding another job, while giving yourself very little chance of resolving it.

4. *'I'm no good without a job. I'm a failure.'*

Question: Is it logical?

Answer: No. You arbitrarily define yourself as good if you have a job, and no good if you don't. There is no necessary logical connection between having a job and feeling that you are a worthwhile person.

Besides, labelling yourself—your entire person as no good, or, for that matter, as good — according to whether you have a job or not, is an example of overgeneralizing and cannot be logically validated. In effect, you are taking one aspect of yourself — your ability to keep a job — and rating your whole being as good or no good simply on the basis of that one aspect.

Similarly, failing to keep a job does not make you a failure. All you can logically say is, 'I have failed on this occasion to keep my job, but that does not necessarily mean that I will always fail in the future.'

Question: Is it realistic?

Answer: Not at all. Human beings are complex living processes whose worth, or value to themselves, cannot be measured by some external arbitrarily selected standard. It makes sense to rate your behaviour, or your performances, because then you can identify your weaknesses and improve your performance. If you then accept yourself as a fallible human being — too complex to be given a single rating — you will stay with reality and avoid tormenting yourself with unanswerable questions about your intrinsic worth.

Question: Does it help me achieve my goals?

Answer: Thinking you are no good without a job will do nothing to stir you into going out and looking for another job. Even if you overcome your inertia and force yourself to look, you will experience anxiety at the prospect of facing job interviews and being rejected. If you experience this kind of setback it will tend to reinforce your low self-worth and encourage you to procrastinate even more concerning looking for jobs.

Once you see why these iBs cannot be upheld you will start to replace them with rBs. These will be somewhat similar to the rBs listed in Table 2, but expressed in a more general form. Thus:

Rational Alternative Beliefs

- 'There's no reason why it should not have happened. If it happens, it happens because the conditions for it to happen were in place.'

- 'It's bad that I've lost my job, but hardly awful or terrible. There are degrees of hardship and inconvenience associated with being made redundant, but I can tolerate that without having to like it.'

- 'I find it unpleasant and a pain in the neck to be made redundant, But I can certainly stand it. In fact, I can stand anything until I am actually dead!'

- 'Who says I'll never get another job? World market conditions are changing all the time, and with it the opportunities for finding new and interesting work.

- 'I certainly derive satisfaction from doing a good job, and I feel inconvenienced by being without one, but my worth to myself is not dependent upon the job I lost or any other job I might have in the future. I can still enjoy my life. I have many aspects to my being, and I, my totality, will never be rateable, although my deeds and performances may be.'

This has been a fairly brief introduction to REBT, but it has not been possible to cover every aspect of this method here.

In the following chapters of this book we will offer you some unusually deep insights into human emotions and behaviour, as well as opportunities to practise your emerging tough-minded skills. Read carefully what we have written in this introduction and think about it frequently. It may sound simple, but it is not so easy to put into practice — especially if much of the material is new to you. What you are basically trying to do is to acquire new habits, and that takes time and practice. We can encourage you to practise, and give you opportunities to do so, but *you* will have to supply the time. Good luck!

TWO

Coping When Others Criticise You

$\mathcal{W}$ho enjoys being criticised? We don't exactly leap with joy when our faults and failings are brought to our attention. Even when the criticism contains at least a grain of truth, we are often loathe to admit it.

You can act in a tough-minded and emotionally healthy way when someone criticises you; you don't have to lose your cool and experience the emotional 'wobblies'!

How do you react when somebody criticises you? If you are like most of us, you probably don't react too well. After all, who enjoys being criticised? We don't exactly leap with joy when our faults and failings are brought to our attention. Even when the criticisms contain at least a grain of truth, we are often loath to admit it. Perhaps we feel put down and wish that our critic had remained silent. Perhaps we defensively refuse to acknowledge that our critic may have a point, and attempt to ignore the criticism by 'clamming up' and remaining silent, or even going into a sulk.

These reactions, while not exactly helpful or in your best interest are not likely to land you in serious trouble. Most people come out of a sulk within a reasonable period of time. However, worse problems tend to emerge when you react angrily to any kind of criticism, however minor. Some people are so 'touchy' that they explode with anger at even a suggestion that they might be in the wrong. Others feel so 'hurt' at being told that their behaviour leaves a lot to be desired, that they may feel quite depressed and sulk for days on end.

Fortunately, you don't have to react in any of these self-defeating ways, regardless of the kind of criticism directed at you. In other words, you can act in a tough-minded and emotionally healthy way when someone criticises you; you don't have to lose your cool and experience the emotional 'wobblies'.

Once you learn how to neither underreact nor overreact to being criticised, and replace your negative feelings with healthier ones, you will find that you can extract the maximum benefit from well-intended criticism. You can also respond appropriately to criticism that is ill-intentioned or misconceived. Let's take a closer look now at some of the ways people upset themselves when others criticise them, or even when they imagine others are criticising them.

Overcoming 'Going-on-the-defensive' Reaction

When people become defensive, instead of honestly owning up to their failings or acknowledging that there may be some truth in their critic's allegations, they shy away from thinking through the implications of the criticism. This is because it would be too 'hurtful' to their self-esteem to admit that the criticisms might be true. To protect themselves from the uncomfortable feelings that stem from an admission of their failings or shortcomings, these people resort to rationalisations and other 'avoidance tactics' such as denial or lying. For example, a father who constantly criticises and bullies his son, and generally behaves in an autocratic manner towards the boy, will deny that he has a strong urge to act like a dictator, but will insist that he is only criticising for the boy's own good.

Why We Become Defensive

Why do people keep sweeping some of their most important thoughts, feelings, and behaviours under the carpet? By now, having read chapter 1, we will suppose that you have achieved several kinds of awareness:

- That feelings don't spontaneously spring into existence or overwhelm you, but that people who experience the feelings *choose* to create and sustain them.

- That people's feelings normally arise from their specific belief systems, from the strong evaluations they have about the things they experience and what they tell themselves about the experiences that occur in their lives.

- That if people's feelings and behaviours are bringing them results they don't want and that are distinctly unhelpful, these people almost invariably have included in their belief systems some distinct and identifiable irrational (i.e. illogical and/or unrealistic) ideas, and that there exists a direct connection between the disturbed feelings and their irrational ideas (REBT Insight No. 1, see page 12).

- And finally, that when people hold iBs that they see are leading to their disturbed feelings and inappropriate behaviours, they can almost always challenge and dispute their iBs and replace them with saner beliefs that will lead to healthier and less self-defeating emotional-behavioural consequences.

So, equipped with these levels of awareness, what iBs would you be looking for when defensiveness gets in the way of enabling you to respond to criticism in a tough-minded manner? Remember, defensiveness is a set of manoeuvers designed to help you to avoid facing unpleasant realities. We gave you a clue when we stated that defences largely stem from self-condemnation. What sort of beliefs would you be holding that would lead you to condemn yourself? Look for the 'musts' and the 'awfulising' that you know by now constitute the essence of iBs.

Irrational Belief Behind Defensive Reactions. We suggest the following iBs would typically be held by people who damn themselves for some socially criticisable behaviour, and who resort to various kinds of defences to keep this behaviour out of their consciousness:

'I must not be disapproved of or criticised by significant people in my life; it's awful when I am disapproved of or criticised, and therefore I am no good.'

There are three Major Irrational Beliefs which, between them, constitute the essence of virtually all emotional problems. You will meet all three of them or their variants as you proceed through this book. Meanwhile, we have outlined Major Irrational Belief No. 1 (see page 35), which you will encounter in one form or another on innumerable occasions.

The iB that we have just identified as lying at the root of self-condemnations is repeated here for easy comparison with Major Irrational Belief No. 1: 'I must not be disapproved of or criticised by significant people in my life; it's awful when I am disapproved of or criticised, and therefore I am no good.' Can you see that this iB is variant of Major Irrational Belief No. 1? If you start off implicitly believing Major Irrational Belief No. 1, then when you are disapproved of or criticised, you take this as 'proof' that you are no longer competent and/or loved. However, since you define not being competent and/or loved as awful and proof that you are worthless, you easily and 'logically' conclude that, whatever happens, you must not be criticised!

Challenging 'Going-on-the-defensive' Response to Criticism. Now, before we analyse and dispute this iB, we suggest that you refresh your memory on the criteria for determining whether a given belief is rational or irrational by returning to Chapter 1, page 16, and looking again at Table 1.

Dispute: Now let's apply these criteria to the iB 'I must not be disapproved of or criticised by significant people in my life; it's awful when I am disapproved of or criticised, and therefore I am no good.'

Is this belief logical? No I certainly don't like being criticised, but it doesn't logically follow that I must not be disapproved of or criticised. If I do have some objectionable traits, does that make me a totally worthless person? No way! My traits and my behaviour are only aspects of me, never the whole of me.

Is this belief realistic? Clearly, it is not. If some law of the universe said that I must not be disapproved of or criticised, then I wouldn't be! Since I am criticised by people whom I consider important, then this belief makes no factual sense.

Moreover, I can hardly claim that it is awful or terrible when people criticise me, although I admit that it may be highly uncomfortable. When I call being criticised awful, though, I am viewing it as more than bad — or 101 per cent bad — which, of course, it cannot be, because things can always be worse.

Does this belief help me achieve my goals? Hardly! So long as I demand that significant individuals must not criticise me, I will only needlessly worry myself by dwelling on the 'horror' of incurring criticism. Obviously, constant worrying about some feared event will do nothing to help me achieve my goals.

Developing a Rational Alternative to 'I-must-not-be-Criticised'. Once you surrender your iBs that you must not be criticised, you could uphold quite a different rational alternative set of beliefs which would enable you to listen to any criticism directed at you, to evaluate its relevance and to take whatever action seemed called for. Thus you could believe the following:

'I prefer not to be criticised by significant others in my life, but there is no reason why I must not be criticised. Criticism can be helpful when offered in a constructive manner; but even when it is not, or when it is intentionally malicious, it is not awful. It is merely a pain in the neck that I can bear.

My traits, deeds, and performances are only aspects of me, not my totality. These aspects may be objectively rated or criticised, but my personal worth as a human being is unaffected. So let me objectively consider the criticisms and try to change those things that I can change, so that I can reach my goals in life and get on better with others.'

With such a rational philosophy, you would no longer feel impelled to deny statements defensively, or possibly suppress the idea that possibly some of your activities and behaviour towards others may be prompted by motives that are quite different from those you would like to believe you have.

Overcoming Anger at Being Criticised

Anger at being criticised is our second example of how a disturbed emotional response can block one's ability to make a rational response to criticism.

Developing 'Tough-minded' Philosophy
Major Irrational Beliefs
which cause Emotional Roadblocks

Major Irrational Belief No. 1
'Because it would be highly preferable if I were outstandingly competent and/or loved, I absolutely *should* and *must* be that. It's awful when I am not, and therefore I am a worthless individual.'

Major Irrational Belief No. 2
'Because it is preferable that others treat me considerately and fairly, they absolutely *should* and *must*; and they are rotten people who deserve to be damned when they do not.'

Major Irrational Belief No. 3
'My life conditions *must* give me the things I *want* and I have to have without too much effort, or else life is unbearable and I *can't* be happy at all!'

Julie worked as a personal secretary to the manager of a small business. While Julie's boss appreciated that Julie's work generally was satisfactory, he did notice that sometimes her typing was rather careless. He had already drawn Julie's attention to this on more than one occasion.

One day Julie handed her boss a letter that she had typed. He glanced through the letter and said 'Your work is sloppy, and you really need to take more care when typing letters.'

Julie heard her boss out in silence, but inwardly she was fuming with anger. As soon as she thought her boss was out of earshot, Julie turned to her colleagues and exclaimed, 'He's got no right to criticise me like that! Who does he think he is! Mr Perfect? That's a laugh! I've had enough of being made the scapegoat in this office, so damn him!' The boss happened to overhear Julie's outburst, and shortly afterwards she found herself looking for another job.

Why People Become Angry at Being Criticised

What was irrational about Julie's reaction to being criticised? Wasn't it an overreaction? Let's look at the facts: Julie is clearly angry and chooses to get even with her boss 'in absentia', by responding with damning criticism of him. She does this in front of office colleagues. Julie's basic anger-creating iB is: 'You must not criticise me, and you are damnable for doing so!' This iB is a variant of Major Irrational Belief No. 2 (see page 35).

Challenging Angry Response to Criticism. *Dispute:* In Chapter 1 (page 21) you will remember we listed three criteria by which you can determine the validity of a belief:

Is it logical?

Is it realistic?

Does it help me achieve my goals?

If you consistently apply these criteria to iBs, you will readily see why these beliefs are irrational and how they can be replaced by rational alternative convictions that are more likely to serve your intrests better.

So let's illustrate how Julie's iBs about being criticised can be Disputed, using the three criteria outlined above:

Is this belief logical? Julie believes that her boss has no right to criticise her. Does that belief stand up to scrutiny? As the boss, he surely has the right to criticise her work. Obviously Julie doesn't like being criticised, but does it logically follow that she must not be criticised because she doesn't like it? It clearly does not follow.

Is this belief realistic? Even if we had a consensus that Julie had been unfairly picked out for criticism of her work, is there some law that says that we must be treated fairly at all times? Obviously, no such law exists. Sometimes we may be treated fairly, sometimes not. It makes no sense to demand that something should not exist that undoubtedly does exist.

Does this belief help Julie achieve her goals? Her refusal to accept criticism and her condemning attitude towards her boss will hardly result in her being supplied with a glowing reference to take to her next job. And so long as she clings to her iB that she must not be criticised for her work, Julie is likely to get herself into trouble on other occasions in any future employment.

A Rational Alternative to Anger

'I definitely don't like being criticised, but there is no reason why I shouldn't be. Any boss I work for has the right to criticise my work. Instead of getting uptight, let me see what the criticism is actually about. If I am doing a poor job in certain respects, it will do me no harm to correct my shortcomings. I can either decide to stay in the situation and lump it, or I can leave and find myself a more congenial employment. In neither event do I have to upset myself needlessly.'

Overcoming 'I am-no-good-if-I am-criticised' Response

If you don't get approval from some significant person in your personal or business life, and you believe you absolutely have to get their approval, you will experience emotional and behavioural problems. The main reason for this is that you hold the iB 'I absolutely need your approval.'

Challenging the 'I am-no-good...' Response. If you hold this iB, then whenever you detect even the slightest hint of criticism or disapproval from the person whose approval you 'need', your alarm bells start ringing. You interpret this as a sign that you are no longer getting the approval that you believe you need. What would that mean for you? Hint: look again at Major Irrational Belief No. 1 on page 35, of which 'I need your approval' is a variant. If you desperately need someone's approval and you don't get it, you conclude you are no good.

And as if feeling you are worthless without someone's guarantee of approval was not bad enough, you may also fear criticism if you strongly hold two other iBs. These are:

'I must get what I want';
'Life must not be too hard'.

In other words, you cling to the idea that you need approval from some special person, since you see lack of approval as a threat to getting what you want in the first case, and a threat to a relatively easy life in the second.

If you want to be tough-minded in the way you handle criticism, you could help yourself by surrendering the absurd notion that you absolutely need the approval of significant people in order to have a reasonably happy existence. So, let's dispute the iBs we identified above:

1. 'I must get what I want'.

Is this belief logical? It's OK to want what you want, but where is the evidence that you must get what you want? It does not follow that because you want something, therefore you must get it.

Is this belief realistic? If there was some law of the universe that stated we must get what we want, then wouldn't we be bound always to get it? But clearly we do not dictate how the universe is run.

Does this belief help you achieve your goals? When you find, that you do not invariably get what you insist you must have, your reaction will tend to be one of anger or self-pity. In neither event will your irrational demands motivate you to look for more rational alternatives to achieving your goals.

A Rational Alternative to 'I am-no-good...'

'I very much prefer to get what I want, both in my personal and my working life, but there is no reason why I absolutely have to. If I am disappointed in one or other respect, that is disadvantageous, but I can still lead a reasonably happy existence even if I never get everything I want.'

Now let's examine the second iB:

2. 'Life must not be too hard'

If you believe this, you will tend to look constantly for signs of approval from whomever you see as holding the key to the easy life you seek. This person may be a potential life partner, spouse, or your boss at the workplace. Thus if you don't get signs of approval, you may be scared that you may have to carry on working much longer than you had anticipated to get the things you want quickly and easily and that would be 'terrible'!

Is this belief logical? Just because you want certain things without having to work too hard to get them, does it logically follow that the world must oblige you? If a thing is difficult, though, it's difficult. Tough!

Is this belief realistic? The facts speak for themselves. Life can be hard, and a great deal harder for some people than others. Is there some law that the world must make life less hard for me? Clearly such a law does not exist, so it makes no sense to demand that it absolutely should!

Does this belief help you achieve your goals? The more I dwell on the unfairness of life being hard, the harder it will seem. This obviously won't help me to achieve my goals of having things easy, since those who might be disposed to help me may well be turned off by my constant demands that life must not be hard for me!

Developing a Rational Alternative to 'Life-must-not -be-too-hard'.

'Whether we like it or not, life can be, and often is, difficult. That's the way it is! If I encounter difficulty in getting some of the things I want out of life, that

40

is unfortunate and frustrating. However, it's not the end of the world, and if working harder or waiting longer for the right person to turn up in my life looks like being the answer, then I had better uncomplainingly do just that. I may not like it, but I can certainly stand it.'

It's worth pointing out that the two iBs we have just disputed are variants of Major Irrational Belief No. 3 (see page 35).

You have now met the three Major Irrational Beliefs, which together form a pool from which virtually all emotional disturbances are derived. As we pointed out earlier, you will seldom meet these Major Irrational Beliefs in their pure or standard form. In practice you will discover variants or derivatives of them, and find that these lie at the root of most of the examples of dysfunctional behaviour and emotional disturbance you are likely to meet.

When disputing your own and other people's iBs, do so vigorously and persistently. Our iBs have become habitual ways of thinking over a long period and are not likely to be wiped out after only a few disputations. You will find that these habitual ways tend to 're-seed' unless you have replaced them with rational convictions that you put into practice. That is the secret of becoming tough-minded: practise uprooting your iBs, and practise acting on your new rational or tough-minded attitudes until they really sink in and become a part of you.

Overcoming 'Hurt' Reaction to Criticism

When you feel hurt concerning comments that seem to you to be uncaring, your reaction is often some kind of withdrawal, accompanied by a closing down of

41

communication with the person who uttered the 'hurtful' remarks. As a result of this communication breakdown, the point at issue fails to get discussed and a number of accusations and counter-accusations may take place before the matter that is of real concern is finally brought into the open.

Jenny and her husband, Tom, were having dinner one evening at home and they had invited Tom's mother to join them. Since Jenny had only limited experience of cooking, dinner usually consisted of a main course of something fairly easy to cook, followed by cheese and biscuits. It was understood between Jenny and Tom that the less said in public about Jenny's experience with cooking, the better.

On this occasion, though, Tom turned to his mother and said in a jocular aside, 'I'm afraid it's just cheese and biscuits for dessert tonight, Mum. Jenny is hopeless when it comes to preparing desserts.' Tom's mother waved away the apology with a laugh, but Jenny wasn't laughing. She hardly spoke a word for the rest of the evening.

When Tom's mother had gone, he said 'What's the matter with you? You've been in a sulk practically all evening and my mother noticed it, too.' Jenny's response was, 'If you really cared about me, you would know what you did to hurt me!' In Jenny's view, Tom had acted uncaringly towards her by making joking remarks about her lack of culinary expertise, a thing he should not have done—especially in front of his mother.

Jenny's basic iB in this case is:

'Since I treat his feelings with consideration, he must reciprocate. It's terrible to be treated in this uncaring manner. He is an inconsiderate and bad person for betraying me in this way.'

Observe that Jenny's feelings are a combination of anger and hurt. Her behavioural response to Tom's behaviour—her sulking—is an indirect way of punishing him for his behaviour and an attempt to make him feel guilty.

Dispute: Jenny is telling herself, 'Since I treat his feelings with consideration, he must reciprocate.' That's the first part. Does that sound rational to you? Let's see.

Is this belief logical? It would be nice if Jenny's husband treated her feelings with the consideration she demands, but why must he for no other reason than that she treats his feelings with consideration? This doesn't logically follow.

Is this belief realistic? Is there was some law that people must treat us as considerately as we treat them? We can all cite instances when our considerate treatment of other people was not matched by their reciprocal treatment of us.

Next, take Jenny's 'It's terrible to be treated in this uncaring manner, particularly as I do not deserve it.' Even if Jenny had, in fact, been treated in an uncaring way, where is the evidence that being treated that way is 'terrible'? It may be sad and regrettable, but is it truly terrible? Can Jenny's treatment be *that* bad?

Finally, Jenny damns her husband as an inconsiderate, bad person for what she regards as a betrayal of trust about her culinary shortcomings. Granted that he acted thoughtlessly, but does that make him an inconsiderate, bad person? If he were, he would act like an inconsiderate bad person at all times. Obviously this is a gross exaggeration.

Do Jenny's beliefs help her achieve her goals? Almost certainly not. Damning other people is hardly the best way to win their cooperation in changing some aspects of their behaviour. Jenny wants her husband to be more considerate. At first, her sulking might encourage her husband to feel guilty, which would then dispose him to watch constantly what he said in case some chance remark triggered another bout of sulking. A better solution would be to show Jenny how she needlessly upsets herself over her husband's sometimes less than perfect behaviour and how, by adopting a more rational attitude towards his occasional inconsiderate behaviour, she could help her husband become more considerate of her feelings.

Jenny's rational alternative belief to 'Since I treat his feelings with consideration, he must reciprocate'. 'I very much want my husband to treat me fairly and with consideration, especially with regard to my shortcomings.

'It's bad, but not terrible when he inconsiderately mentions something in company that we had agreed would be kept between ourselves. I'll never like it when he acts in this manner, but I can certainly stand it.

'He isn't a worthless person, but a fallible human being who has a tendency to act inconsiderately at times.'

With this set of rBs, Jenny can then inform her husband that she does not like his occasionally inconsiderate behaviour, and that if he were substantially to reduce the frequency of such occurrences, she would view his efforts as a significant step towards improving the quality of their relationship.

Here you see how substituting a feeling of annoyance instead of angry hurt activates her to try to change her situation, whereas her old feelings of hurt and anger encourage her to engage in sulky withdrawal.

Analysing Criticism

So far, we've been examining some of the major ways in which many people needlessly upset themselves when responding to criticism, and which effectively sabotage their chances of potentially benefiting from the criticism. This can occur even when the criticism is well-intentioned, and aimed at helping the individual to improve some aspect of his or her performance at work.

If you have taken in what we have said so far, and are able to listen to criticism without fearing disapproval, regardless of whether the criticism is spot on or wide off the mark, you are now in a position to spot the irrationalities in other people's criticism and hopefully, help them to identify and challenge their irrational ideas. A word of warning, though! Your objective is to determine if the criticism directed at you has some degree of truth in it and then to take the appropriate action. We are *not* advocating that you pinpoint other people's irrationalities in order to be 'one up' on them. That in itself would be irrational. Show your critic that you unconditionally accept him or her as a person, and that you are only criticising the irrational ideas behind their criticism of you, with a view to clarifying its content.

Keep Talking! Don't lose sight of the importance of keeping your communication channels open at all times between you and your critics. Once communication breaks down, the chances are that at least one of you is in the grip of one or more Major Irrational Beliefs, along with the disturbed emotional and behavioural reactions that stem from them.

Let's assume that you have achieved a reasonable degree of success in identifying and disputing your own iBs, and are eager to see how you cope when others criticise you. You agreed that you had shortcomings of your own when these were pointed out to you, and you were not afraid to admit it. You can take criticism without feeling angry or hurt. So let us move on now and take a hard look at what people may be trying to tell you when they criticise you.

Constructive Criticism can be Good

In previous sections we have pointed out that you can often benefit from criticism if you view it as an opportunity of being provided with useful feedback on how you could improve your ideas and/or performance. This applies regardless of which area of your life is targeted for criticism.

For example, you may be interested in getting feedback from your tennis coach on how you could improve your service; or you may welcome constructive suggestions from your company's appraisement officer on how you could better your performance; or you might be interested in receiving hints from your partner on how you could improve as a lover. In each case, the point to remember is that you can try to improve your performances once you realise that any criticism you receive is a criticism only of your ideas, deeds, or performances — never of you as a person.

Being criticised doesn't invalidate you as a person; your personal worth to yourself is not at stake. This follows from the contention that we will continue to reiterate throughout this book: that we can only legitimately rate a person's deeds, traits, ideas, and behaviours — never the person herself or himself.

Constructive and Unconstructive Criticism. Basically there are two kinds of criticism — constructive and unconstructive:

Constructive criticism. This is usually offered by a person who takes responsibility for it. This can range from critical evaluations of your performance at work to legitimate complaints from a person who has suffered inconvenience or damage due to negligence or carelessness on your part. It is unlikely to be in your best interests to ignore such criticism, or legitimate complaints. Accept yourself as a fallible human being who will make mistakes and commit errors of judgement from time to time and work out how to avoid making those mistakes in future.

Unconstructive criticism. In this category we include chronic complainers and fault-finders who have an axe to grind, and whose constant criticism may be aimed at getting rid of your presence.

This may happen in an office if you are seen as a threat to someone's promotion. Or maybe a mother will try to manipulate her daughter's feelings in order to make her look after her mother in old age. In general, people in this category use criticism as a means of expressing their own agenda, and are not at all interested in offering helpful criticism.

However, the following sections will provide you with some useful ideas to help you cope when you come up against people who, for one reason or another, may make life difficult for you.

Coping with Chronic Complainer

To cope successfully with chronic complainers, it helps to understand them — to know what lies behind their actions and to avoid being sucked into their accusatory game. Such people often have a gigantic chip on their shoulders. Chronic complainers are whiners; they gripe *ad nauseam* about anything and everything. Believing themselves to be powerless to take control of their own lives, these people firmly believe the world *should be* this way, or *should not be* that way, and that you and/or other people should do something about it!

One way to find out what such a complainer appears to be upset about is first to listen attentively, and acknowledge that you understand how that person feels. Then, without being defensive or agreeing with the complainer you proceed to ask the other person, 'What precisely do you think I'm not doing right?' or, 'What precisely do you think I can do about it?' Have you tried doing something yourself to change the situation?' Encourage the other person to be specific, to answer the question, 'What precisely are you criticising me for?' If you get a straight answer, at least you have identified something specific you can look at next.

Often you won't get a straight answer. Instead, you will sometimes get a whole string of overgeneralisations and exaggerations — things like, 'You *never* do this' or 'You are *always* doing that'. Chronic complainers are fond of words like 'always' and 'never'. You may get specific complaints, or at other times your critic talks in terms of your traits, rather than offering you specific examples of your alleged acts of commission or omission. Let's consider this example from a family situation.

'Nobody ever comes to see me': A case study

Sarah, a 50-year-old divorcee living alone, would complain how her 75-year-old mother was constantly demanding attention from her family. The mother, who rented a private room in a warden-controlled block of flats for the elderly, did not enjoy good health — *and* made the most of it. She claimed that she couldn't write to friends because her hand shook, and she couldn't visit anyone because she felt unsteady on her feet. Whenever Sarah took her mother out to a restaurant the occasion was often marred by the mother's constant grumbling and complaints about how ungrateful her family was. As Sarah observed, 'My mother is her own worst enemy. We'd all want to spend more time with her if she'd just stop criticising us and reminding us of how much she did for us when we were little.'

After a time, Sarah and her brothers became wise to their mother's manipulative ploys; but at first, Sarah would feel angry with her mother. 'I do my best for her,' said Sarah, 'I've offered many times to take her home with me and stay, but she always refuses.' See if you can detect the implicit iBs in Sarah's thinking whenever she felt angry with her mother. They would be something like: 'It's *awful* that she criticises us constantly!' and 'She absolutely shouldn't treat us as if we were still just her kids!'

Whenever the mother saw that Sarah was angry with her, she would not telephone or respond to letters. Sarah would then feel guilty, and wonder if something had happened to her mother, and would end up by making a special journey to see her. As soon as Sarah stepped inside her mother's room, she invariably saw that there was nothing wrong with her. Her mother however, never seemed surprised to see Sarah. She would then take Sarah's visit as a sign that she was sorry for getting angry. Then her grousing would begin all over again.

Eventually, Sarah realised how she was allowing her mother to manipulate her feelings, and was then able to listen to her mother's barrage of complaints without upsetting herself.

Sarah felt sorry that her mother seemed unable to appreciate that she and the other members of the family had their own lives to live, but that this in no way implied that they no longer cared about their mother. But if that was the way her mother was, and would continue to be, tough!

What iBs do you think underpinned the mother's continual faultfinding and self-pity? Probably they consisted of a few variants of Major Irrational Belief No. 3.

'My family *should* treat me better than they do; it's awful that they don't and I can't stand their ingratitude.'

You have already come across a variant of Major Irrational Belief No. 3 in the case of Jenny, which we discussed earlier. The example shown here is another instance.

What do you think Sarah could do to improve her relationship with her mother? The answer is, probably not too much in the way of changing her mother's iBs. Her mother has been firmly wedded to her irrational convictions for a long time, and it is unlikely she will be persuaded to give them up. However, Sarah could show her mother that each of them sees things somewhat differently, and that she does not accept her mother's allegations of indifference or neglect. Nevertheless she can emphatically convey that she unconditionally accepts her mother just as she is. In order to feel that way, what would Sarah's rBs be about her mother's general attitude?

Sarah's Rational Alternative Beliefs About Being Criticised. Once Sarah had overcome her earlier tendency to get angry concerning her mother's continual fault-finding, she could rationally believe the following:

> 'I wish my mother would stop her continual criticism but there is no reason why she has to. She sees her situation from her own perspective and responds to what goes on in her own mind. Her constant criticism is irritating. Her apparent lack of appreciation is disappointing. However, we can stand it, even though we'll never like it. Our mother may never change her perceptions of her family, but we can unconditionally accept her with her failings and continue to show her that we care for her despite her negative views.'

Once Sarah's mother could see that her daughter accepted her as a person, and in spite of being criticised was able to show her acceptance by taking a continuing interest in her mother's welfare — then Sarah's mother might eventually become less critical and more appreciative.

You will appreciate now why it is important that Sarah does not react to her mother's criticism angrily, as she occasionally did at first. This would tend to reinforce her mother's perceptions that her criticisms of her family were justified. The result would be a still further deterioration in the relationship between Sarah's mother and her family.

Coping with a Difficult Interview at Work

'You'll never change!' We have stated that criticism can be helpful. In an office or workplace, the intention behind criticism, is to draw your attention to your shortcomings and suggest how you could raise the standard of your overall performance. In appraisement for promotion interviews, the interviewer usually goes beyond criticising your performance and is more interested in assessing your potential for progress within the organisation.

Bosses, supervisors, and interviewers are human, and probably hold a number of iBs. Here are a few pointers to help you get onto your interviewer's wavelength and help yourself in the bargain:

- When you receive criticism, ask yourself what is being criticised. Don't accept vague generalities, such as 'you'll never change'; seek clarification. Ask your interviewer to be specific. 'What is it about me that you think will never change? Or, 'What precisely am I being criticised for?' If you get a specific complaint, ask yourself, 'Are they right?' If so, admit it, and then say, 'OK, this is something I can work on and try to correct, so that I do better in the future.'

- If specific points are raised about your performance, welcome them! Intelligent criticism gives you an opportunity to see how others objectively view your performance and potential for further promotion, and can help you to change those aspects of your performance or general attitude that are seen as unhelpful.

- If words like 'hopelessly incompetent' or other such expressions are directed at you, swallow your displeasure and try to get your interviewer to be more specific and say exactly what he or she means.

- Look for what the other person is really concerned with. See whether it is good useful feedback on your performance, an expression of the other person's agenda, or an indication of personal prejudice. For example, if you are female and your interviewer is male, you may sometimes detect a sexist overtone in a remark or question directed at you. If your interviewer says, 'If we gave you this promotion, what guarantee have we that you won't give it up after a few months, say, to start a family?', you could respond with, 'There are no guarantees that anyone — male or female — taking this promotion will still be there in six months' time. There are all sorts of reasons why someone might leave. You would not ask a male promotee that question, so why are you asking me for a guarantee?'

Developing Sensitivity to Criticism

If you are oversensitive to criticism, you will tend to overestimate the extent of the severity of the criticisms you receive. Some people see criticism where none is intended. This hypersensitivity springs from having a low opinion of oneself and imagining that other people agree with it.

Nobody is perfect, and interviewers are fallible like the rest of us. What, rationally speaking, you will be looking for in a job appraisement interview is constructive, objectively offered, verifiable criticism — information that you can use to achieve your goals.

Skilled interviewers will often be helpful to you if you listen carefully to what they are saying and trying to convey to you.

People are Overcritical. Some interviewers may be reluctant to give praise even when the standard of your work has merited it. If you receive nothing but negative criticism, it may be because your interviewer may consider that giving ostensible approval or praise is tantamount to encouraging you to take it easy, or to try less hard in the future. Perfectionists sometimes take this view. Perfectionism is a legitimate aim in your work performance, but when you do exceptionally well, that doesn't make you an exceptionally good person.

Don't inflate your 'ego' by rating yourself as perfect when you do an exceptionally good piece of work. Some interviewers may make this irrational connection and view you and your acts as being the same thing. Knowing this, you can make allowances, and avoid becoming unduly dismayed by your interviewer's apparent lack of appreciation of your sterling performances at work.

When People are not Critical Enough. Normally, interviewers will not shrink from making cogent criticisms of your abilities and job performances. That is what they are there for, and it is usually in your best interests to listen carefully to what they say.

Occasionally, though, you may encounter an interviewer who is somewhat inhibited about being directly critical. They are afraid you might feel upset if they are too direct in their criticisms, so they tactfully soft-pedal their critical comments in the hope that you won't feel 'hurt' if they have to point out.

Here, the error is the opposite of the error made by the perfectionist. The perfectionist errs on the side of being over critical, and the 'too nice' interviewer errs on the side of not being critical enough.

Your objective should be to make each appraisement interview a useful learning experience. If it fails to achieve that, you have really wasted your time. If you consider that your interviewer is letting you off too lightly, you can help by acknowledging your own failures and shortcomings. This may help your interviewer to be more forthcoming, and more specific in assessing your potential for promotion.

One final point. Our ideas and our performances can be criticised. They can be rated good, bad, or indifferent, and we can learn useful things from good feedback. If you are oversensitive you will tend to miss the salient part of the criticism because you will no longer be listening to it. Instead, you will be dwelling upon the 'terrible' things that you think are being said about you!

Focus your attention upon what is being criticised. If you are called incompetent, extract what it was you did, or did not do, that showed incompetence. If you are called a hopeless individual, your critic is wrong because total self-rating is not legitimate. There's no need to be afraid of intelligent appraisal and criticism. Once you take the 'horror' out of being criticised, then intelligent, well-intentioned criticism can be a good thing if used constructively to improve your performance and achieve your goals.

THREE

Expressing Healthy Criticism

*O*ur aim is to show you how to identify and combat your own unconstructive negative reactions to (difficult) people when they respond to you in negative, unhelpful ways.

$\mathcal{I}$n this chapter we will show you how to express criticism in a manner likely to increase your chances of getting the kind of healthy, positive responses you want from people, while minimising the kind of negative responses you don't want. Since there would be little point in discussing how to criticise people who are easy to get through to, and who, for the most part, will readily accept your criticisms, our main focus will be on those issues that have to be considered when you need to criticise the behaviour of 'difficult people'.

When we use the term 'Difficult People' we are not in any sense labelling certain people as intrinsically, or always, 'difficult'. The term 'Difficult People', which will appear without the inverted commas from here on, is used as a shorthand description of people who at times, or in certain circumstances, react negatively in ways that makes it difficult to sustain constructive communication with them.

Who and What are Difficult People?

The answer to the first part of that question is 'virtually all of us'. We can all be difficult to communicate with at times. Looked at from our own point of view, Difficult People are people who, when offered constructive criticism, respond in an awkward, inappropriate, or unconstructive way.

Bear in mind that your object is not to try to change Difficult People. You can't change people because people respond to what is going on in their own minds rather than what is in yours.

Your object is to learn how to identify and overcome those emotional blocks of your own that can seriously interfere with your ability to express criticism of their behaviour in an effective manner. Once you upset yourself about the attitudes of these people, the task of getting your points across to them becomes appreciably more difficult. In an interaction between two people where only one party is being difficult, securing some kind of working agreement is hard enough; if both parties are being 'difficult' — that is, behaving in a way that blocks mutual communication and understanding — the chances of a mutually acceptable outcome are almost nil.

So-called Difficult People are not a race apart, but simply people like ourselves who sometimes, or often, have difficulty in thinking straight and exhibit unhealthy negative feelings and self-defeating patterns of behaviour.

So, let's begin with ourselves. Our aim is to show you how to identify and combat your own unconstructive negative reactions to Difficult People when they respond to you in negative, unhelpful ways.

People are Not Difficult, They Only Act Difficult (Focus on the Act, not the Person)

Focusing on the person's acts doesn't mean that you totally ignore the person. Acts don't get done by themselves, but by people. While you are going to focus primarily on the act or behaviour, you need to remain aware that the person is responsible for the act or behaviour. While you can evaluate an individual's traits, acts, performances, and behaviour, you cannot legitimately evaluate a person, because a person is an ongoing ever-changing process and too complex to be capable of being given an overall rating. Thus, while you could give a person's ability to play badminton or write reports some kind of a score based on a scale of measurement, you could not give the person herself or himself an overall score.

Not everyone appreciates this distinction between rating a person and rating that person's traits or abilities. It is therefore important that when you are criticising someone's performance at work, for example, that you make that distinction clear to the person you are criticising. Otherwise, she/he may take the criticism personally, and interpret your remarks as an attack upon them. As a result, the recipient of your critical remarks may clam up defensively and give you no indication of how they intend to behave in future; or they may get angry and deny the substance of your criticism as a way of protecting their ego from the 'insult' implied by your critical comments.

Since you may have no prior knowledge of how the person is likely to react to criticism, you can usefully begin by tactfully informing the person that any criticism you may make is not to be taken as an attack on them personally. Present it instead as an opportunity for the person to use the information you are providing as valuable feedback on his or her strengths and weaknesses. This leads logically into a discussion of ways and means that the person can use to improve his or her performance.

These remarks apply with equal force to personal, family, and community situations. You may think you know someone well enough to believe that any constructive criticism you offer is likely to be accepted in the spirit in which you intend it, but don't give them the benefit of the doubt! Make it clear to the other person at the outset that you are only criticising some aspect of his or her behaviour that you find unacceptable, and not lambasting the doer of the deed.

Combating Your Own Negative Reactions to People Who Act Difficult

Let's suppose that it is your function to appraise people's job performance, and to assess their suitability for promotion. Some of your interviewees are subordinates in your departments, while others come from other departments within the organisation. It would be nice if everyone you criticised listened attentively to what you had to say, then responded with, 'I really appreciate what you've just told me about my job performance. I hadn't realised that my performance in certain areas was less than expected of me. I fully intend to work hard to correct them. Would you care to offer me some advice on how I could best go about doing that?'

Unfortunately, you will quite often receive a different response from your interviewee — or even none at all! Let's suppose that the individual whose performance record at work you are criticising refuses to accept your evaluation of his performance. Instead he argues back, goes into lengthy explanations, blames other departments or individuals for his failures, and tries to get you involved in a war of words. You do your best to get your interviewee to stick to the point, to focus on the facts recorded in his performance record, but to no avail. You realise you have wasted an hour of your time, and that you have failed to achieve a positive outcome to the interview. You feel angry.

Unfortunately, feeling angry will do little to help you deal effectively with this difficult customer or the next difficult person you encounter. Getting into an angry altercation will only cloud the real issue. The interviewee may well feel that your display of anger justifies his own hostile reaction. You will end the interview without having achieved anything useful.

In this section we shall discuss anger as the first of the three inappropriate negative reactions that you may experience when you are criticising the behaviour or performance of Difficult People during interviews with them. While interview settings at work are chosen to illustrate the points we shall make, our treatment may be readily adapted to other real-life situations — for example, family and domestic scenarios. Now, let's see how we make ourselves angry.

Dealing with 'Difficult People': Controlling your anger

In the case discussed here, the following sequence of events occurs. First, you observe that you are dealing with a difficult person who is belligerent and argumentative. You know that your aim of achieving a satisfactory interview is being frustrated. Secondly, you have a personal rule that interviews are successful only if the other person listens attentively to your criticism, is prepared to acknowledge that they have at least some validity, and that she/he will actively try to do something constructive to improve their performance in the future. By his behaviour, the other person has already violated your rule.

Your anger now arises, not from your inference that the interviewee has frustrated your desire to obtain a satisfactory outcome but rather because of the iBs you hold about your inference. These take the form of 'You must not act in this way, and you are damnable for doing so.'

In the interview context, you are probably holding a fairly specifi- iB about the individual sitting opposite you — namely, 'He's being truculent, argumentative, and frustrating — and he absolutely shouldn't be that way! Damn him!' That's what you believe, but is it a rational belief? Let's see.

Dispute. In Disputing you will recall that we ask three questions to decide whether or not a belief meets the criteria of rationality. So let's apply these three questions to the belief 'He's being truculent, argumentative, and frustrating — and he absolutely shouldn't be that way!'

Is this belief logical? Does it logically follow that because you dislike this man's behaviour therefore he absolutely shouldn't behave in that way? No matter how much you dislike something that exists, there is no logical reason why it must not exist. 'I don't like x, therefore x must not exist!' is quite illogical.

Is it realistic? You may well be correct that your interviewee's behaviour was truculent and uncooperative, but why shouldn't he behave truculently and uncooperatively? That's the way he is! What exists, exists. Therefore it is nonsense to claim that he absolutely shouldn't be the way he is.

Does this belief about your interviewee help you reach your goals? Since the goal is to make each interview a useful and constructive experience for your interviewee, the answer is 'probably not'. Getting angry may elicit from the other person still more hostility and uncooperative behaviour. Also, anger will prevent you from clearly seeing your own mistakes, and the process of establishing a meaningful dialogue with your respondent will be disrupted.

The Rational Alternative to Anger. Once you have seen that your anger-creating beliefs are unsustainable and distinctly unhelpful, you can replace them with rational alternative beliefs such as the following:

> 'This fellow is being difficult, and frustrates me because of his uncooperative behaviour. I would prefer that he didn't do this, but there is no reason why he mustn't be the way he is. Maybe if I keep my cool and show him I'm listening to him, we can lower the temperature and begin to get somewhere.'

Your new feeling in response to these rBs would tend to be annoyance. Thus, when you are annoyed, your tendency is to remain in the situation and deal with it constructively by choosing responses that your experience and training suggest may be effective in eliciting more co-operative behaviour from your interviewee. Without the distorting effects of anger upon your judgement, you are better able to focus on the nature of your interaction with this person, and adopt tactics designed to improve the dialogue. For example, by actively listening to your interviewee's complaints, you may discover that if he had frequently failed to meet his deadlines, for example, it might not be entirely his fault. This might be what he feels upset about being unfairly criticised for lapses in his performance that were really due to circumstances outside his control and that his own boss seemed unaware of.

The main point to be taken here is that by accepting Difficult People the way they are, instead of demanding that they shouldn't be that way, you open up the way to establish a two-way communication which is, after all, one of your objectives.

Dealing with 'Difficult People': Controlling your anxiety

Anxiety is another possible negative reaction that could interfere with your goal of conducting a successful interview when some direct criticism of a person's performance is called for.

Consider the same interview scenario as before, but this time your interviewee is a person of a very different type. Throughout your entire session the interviewee just sits there like a clam, silent and unresponsive. He may be one of those people who have learned that silence is the only way they can handle unpleasant situations such as appraisal interviews. When it becomes clear that you are getting nowhere with this individual, you begin to feel anxious. You try not to show it because you are aware that this unresponsive individual may be deliberately clamming up as a way of expressing resentment at you or the organisation you represent.

It is worth noting that this kind of 'silent treatment' is sometimes also seen in family situations, when one person uses it as a way of getting back at some other family member in order to settle an old score or personal grievance.

Faced with this array of motivations, and having no ready means of telling what the silence means, you wonder what to do. You try to get *some* response from this person sitting in front of you, who is still silently staring at the floor. You've completed your appraisal, and now you say, 'Do you agree with what I've said?', 'Do you think my assessment is fair', or 'Is there anything I should know about your performance or the circumstances under which you have performed your duties that has not been mentioned?' Silence!

At this point you feel really anxious. Since you see your present failure as a blow to your self-worth, you experience 'ego anxiety'.

Let's repeat here what the interviewer believed about his failure to conduct a successful interview with one particular variety of difficult person: 'I absolutely should have been able to get this difficult customer to open up, but instead I've failed completely. Therefore there is something radically wrong with me!'

Dispute: Again, we need to direct our usual sequence of questions to this belief in order to discover if it meets the criteria of rationality. Thus:

Is this belief logical? Well, you tried to get some response from your interviewee, and you certainly wanted to do so. However, it doesn't logically follow that because you wanted to achieve something and tried to achieve it, therefore you should have succeeded.

Moreover, does it logically follow that because you failed in this one instance that there must be something radically wrong with you? Not at all! There could be several other reasons why you failed. For example, your interviewee could have made up his mind to remain silent, regardless of who conducted his interview.

Therefore, your conclusion that there must be something radically wrong with you is invalid.

Is it realistic? No, it is unrealistic. You failed to get this guy to open up; that is a fact.

The fact that you failed is then taken as 'proof' that there is something wrong with you. There is a gross exaggeration in this statement.

Apart from that exaggeration, though, there is an even greater error. It lies in the fact that you equate your self-worth with your ability to conduct a successful interview. As we have already been at pains to emphasise, you can rate your performance and other measurable aspects of your abilities, but you cannot legitimately rate your 'self', your personhood.

Does this belief help me achieve my goals? If your goal is to achieve successful interviews and you continue to cling to the belief that you must succeed with every interview and that you are no good if you don't, we'd certainly bet against you! As soon as you set up 'have to's, 'got to's, or 'shoulds' and apply these to your job performance — or anything else for that matter — and make your self-worth dependent upon succeeding with these demands, you've cooked your goose! You'll rarely be free of anxiety, for anxiety is in some ways a high-class name for low self-acceptance.

The Rational Alternative to Anxiety.

'I wish I had succeeded in persuading my interviewee to open up and respond to my criticisms. It's unfortunate that I failed on this occasion, but it doesn't mean that there is anything radically wrong with me. I am a fallible human being.'

With these rBs, you would still feel concerned about the possibility of encountering other Difficult People of this sort in the future. You might also decide to see how you could improve your diagnostic and communication skills, in order to increase the chances of obtaining a successful outcome on your next challenging assignment.

Dealing with 'Difficult People': Never feel guilty

There are several reasons why you might experience a feeling of guilt when expressing criticism to somebody, especially if your relationship with the person places you in a dominant position.

Imagine you are interviewing a person who is neither hostile nor unresponsive. Instead, this person seems only too ready to accept everything you say as gospel truth. You've really been coming on strong with your criticism, before it dawns on you that this is a weak person who can't stand his ground. 'He's a nice person,' you tell yourself, 'and its best not to upset nice people.' That's your personal code of moral values, and you rightly infer that you have broken your personal moral code. That's what brings on the feeling of guilt. Now, suppose we examine that belief to see if it really stands up. Bear in mind that we are not disputing the fact that you behaved poorly — the reality is that you did break one aspect of your moral code. We're not questioning that. What we are going to examine is what you believe about the fact that you broke your personal code of moral values.

Is this belief logical? The first part says 'I absolutely should not have done what I did.' You have an intention to do or not to do something, but it does not follow

69

that you are bound by an absolute necessity to carry out your intention — or not, as the case may be.

The second part of your belief states, 'I've done a bad thing, therefore I'm damnable and deserve to be punished.' Now let us suppose that you have, in fact, done a bad thing. Does it logically follow that you are damnable? Who says so? Some may damn you because that's their standard; others will forgive you.

Is it realistic? Quite the contrary! You did act in a certain way, so it makes no sense to say that you absolutely should not have acted in that way. Even if we grant that you acted badly, that hardly makes you a damnable person. It would be useful to recall what we said about self-rating: rate the act, not the person!

Does this belief help you attain your goals? It's unlikely that a feeling of guilt will prove highly motivating. You will tend to be preoccupied with undoing the wrong that you did, and this can take several forms. You may be unduly apologetic towards your 'victim', you may bend over backwards to be nice to the extent of soft-pedalling your criticism. All in all, none of these responses would be likely to help you to learn from your mistakes, or to behave in a more helpful manner with future interviewees who are unduly sensitive to criticism.

The Rational Alternative to Guilt.

'I don't like what I did, and I would have preferred not to have helped this nice person to upset himself, but there is no reason why I absolutely should not have done it. I may have made a mistake on this occasion, but I'm not damnable for doing so.'

70

The rational alternative feeling to guilt is remorse. You may still stand by your personal code — that it's best not to upset nice people by being too strong in your criticism of them — but you know that you did not upset that nice person; he upset himself. You accept some measure of responsibility for that, but you don't feel guilty about it. Thus without soft-pedalling you could aim to put your criticisms across more tactfully to this person, while at the same time emphasising that you are criticising only their performance, not their whole person.

Expressing Constructive Criticism: Be spontaneous, be comfortable

Paradoxical though it may sound, you learn how to express constructive criticism comfortably and spontaneously only after you have learned to do it uncomfortably and unspontaneously; and when you do eventually learn to respond to someone's comments, or to express criticism of them spontaneously, it's not all that spontaneous.

When you are spontaneous you very often express destructive criticism. You have to watch your words and be tactful sometimes, if you wish to avoid an angry response from the other person.

You Feel as You Think. In the section where we showed you how to combat your own spontaneous negative reactions to hostile or uncooperative behaviour from Difficult People, you were in effect learning how to question and dispute unspontaneously the iBs underlying your negative reactions, and replace them with spontaneous, rationally thought-out alternatives. In time, and with practice, you may be able to respond spontaneously to the awkward behaviour of Difficult People with rational, mutually helpful and productive counter-strategies. However, it takes time to change one's philosophy and the long-standing habits.

Spontaneity Comes with Practice! Let's suppose that you have decided to learn to become more effective in expressing constructive criticism. To this end you have realised your negative reactions such as anger, anxiety, or guilt when Difficult People are giving you a hard time.

At first, when somebody becomes obstructive or abusive in response to your constructive criticism, you deliberately tell yourself, 'This person sounds upset. Maybe he has a problem. It won't help if I upset myself over this person's behaviour and give him a mouthful. I'd better listen carefully, try to find out what the real problem is, and deal with it as best I can.' That's what you do initially and only after your new REBT way of thinking has become an established habit do you find yourself spontaneously, quickly, and habitually responding tactfully or firmly to achieving a satisfactory outcome to the situation.

Comfort Comes with Practice! Generally speaking, we feel comfortable with what we are used to. We become habituated to something and we find we are comfortable with it. As with spontaneity, you learn to do new or different things 'uncomfortably' at first. However, if you practise doing these new things, eventually you tend to do them unthinkingly and they become comfortable.

Expressing Constructive Criticism: Communicate effectively

This book is not handbook of communication skills. Our aim is to provide you with a good foundation on which you can build as you progress in knowledge and experience. The following sections will provide you with some basic skills to help you communicate constructive or healthy criticism more effectively to Difficult People. First, we emphasise the importance of listening.

Listen Attentively! If you are setting out to criticise someone constructively, such as an office colleague or a subordinate you are usually the one who initiates the conversation. We use the word 'conversation' deliberately, because your object is not simply to give the other person a ticking off for something she/he has, or has not, done.

Criticising someone's performance or behaviour is not an end in itself; constructive criticism has a goal. That goal is to change the way a job is being done, or to change some aspect of a person's performance, or behaviour. Making your criticism specific and factual will therefore help to ensure that the other person does not see your criticism as a personal attack.

To achieve the objective of constructive criticism, you need to discuss what changes will be necessary and how and/or when the other person will implement them. That involves listening attentively to the other person's responses. Has the other person indicated that the content of your criticism has been understood? If not, you may need to repeat and clarify your main points, periodically checking that the meanings you are trying to convey coincide with the meanings being received. In other words, you actively listen!

Active listening also means acknowledging that you have heard the other person, letting that person know that you have understood what they've said and that you know how they feel. You try to receive the meanings, not just the words in their communication. Once you feel that the other person has understood the point of your criticism and that his responses to it have been understood by you, then you can proceed to discuss how the changes you require will be carried out. You have reached the stage of constructive problem-solving.

Expressing Constructive Criticism: The importance of style

There are basically three different styles people use to communicate: assertive, non-assertive, and aggressive. Expressing constructive criticism in an assertive style will usually be more effective than expressing non-assertively or aggressively in situations where it would be more constructive and appropriate to act assertively.

Assertive—the Win-Win Style. Assertion means standing up for your rights, and expressing your opinions, feelings, and preferences in direct, honest, and appropriate ways that respect the rights of the other person(s).

In assertion, you recognise that both you and the other person have rights, opinions, feelings, and preferences, and you aim to satisfy the desires of both parties involved or, at least, reach a satisfactory compromise. You strive for what is termed a 'win-win' situation.

Non-Assertive Style. Non-assertion means failing to stand up for your rights, and expressing your opinions, feelings, and preferences in such a diffident or apologetic way that others can easily disregard them.

Typically in a non-assertive situation you believe that the other person's opinions, feelings, preferences, or desires are more important than your own, that the other person has rights, but you do not, and that your aim is to avoid conflict and please others—or at least, not displease them.

Aggressive Style. Aggression refers to standing up for your rights, but in ways that violate the rights of other people. Aggression means ignoring, dismissing, or belittling the opinions, feelings, preferences and desires of other people, and expressing your own wants, feelings, and opinions in inappropriate or hostile ways.

Your aim in aggression is to win, at others' expense if necessary.

Aggressive vs Assertive: A case study

Let's take a fairly typical situation in a workplace to illustrate the three different options. A subordinate, whose duty it is to furnish you with computer printouts of daily turnover, has been sending incomplete data without any accompanying explanations. You decide to take the matter up.

An Assertive Approach. A constructive criticism delivered in an assertive manner would be:

'Bob, I want to talk to you about the computer printouts you send me of our daily turnover. I've noticed that of late there has been the odd page missing or torn; that makes figures in the summary suspect. Have you noticed this?'

When you have listened to Bob's response, you then might go on to say:

'Why is this happening? What ideas do you have to ensure that we get complete printouts in future? If there are future hiccoughs, can you make sure that I'm advised when that happens and that I'm given a provisional estimate of the daily figures in advance of the final printout?'

Once you have received satisfactory answers you can then summarise the actions to be taken.

With this you have both had your rights respected. You had the right and the responsibility to draw an unsatisfactory aspect of Bob's performance to his attention. He had the right to have the facts given to him in a non-judgemental manner as well as the opportunity to use his expertise to suggest ways to resolve the problem satisfactorily. You constructively criticised a failing in Bob's performance and he was able to take constructive action to remedy it.

A Non-Assertive Approach. A non-assertive approach might start with you telling yourself: 'I don't think Bob's going to like it if I point out that his output has been a bit sloppy lately. Maybe I'd better say nothing and hope that he somehow spots what's wrong and corrects it himself without being told.' When nothing at all changes and you feel forced to confront, you tend to say something like, 'Bob, I wonder if I could have a word? I hate to mention it, Bob, but you know those computer printouts you send me? Well, I'm afraid there's a few things about them that are, well, not quite right.'

By the time you get around to telling Bob just what was wrong with the printouts, he'll have got the impression that it's not all that important an issue.

The outcome is that you feel unhappy that you have to put up with the problem for some undeterminate period, and that this certainly won't make your job any easier. You feel as if you have behaved weakly and ineffectively; you also feel angry at yourself for appearing weak in your own eyes, and probably, you suspect, in Bob's eyes as well.

An Aggressive Approach. An aggressive approach typically involves handling the situation in an abrupt and heavy-handed manner. For example, you walk straight into Bob's office, fling the sheaf of computer printouts on to his desk, and in a loud voice come out with:

'Look at these printouts! What the devil do you think you're doing sending this rubbish to me! It's full of mistakes and missing pages! Don't you bother to check *anything* that leaves your office these days?'

The chances are that Bob will resent your aggressive attitude, resent the fact that you didn't give him a chance to identify the specific problem, and interpret your criticism as a personal attack. The outcome is likely to be resentful compliance with your demand coupled with just the minimum of cooperation from Bob in future. And because of your aggressive approach, important issues concerning a possible need for tighter quality control will tend to be ignored, with knock-on effects to the detriment of the business as a whole.

Why assertion works best. We stated at the beginning of this section that an assertive attitude was likely to be the more effective way of expressing healthy or constructive criticism. If you compare the three points — assertion, non-assertion, and aggression — you will see why.

77

On the basis of these comparisons, it should be clear why assertion is the effective option; you are more likely to communicate constructive criticism effectively to another person when you clearly convey respect for the rights of that person and there is direct, open, and honest expression of opinions, feelings, desires, and preferences.

If you agree that an assertive attitude will help you to be more effective when you wish to express healthy criticism, you may logically ask what you can do to eliminate non-assertive and aggressive attitudes. As a first step, can you recall REBT Insight No. 1, which will give you the clue you need to proceed. Here it is again, for your convenience:

REBT Insight No. 1. You feel the way you think and all your thoughts, feelings, and behaviour are interrelated.

So if we want to change an attitude that seems to be unhelpful, we would do well to look at what we are thinking to create the unhelpful attitude. Let us examine what Ken and Kate Back refer to as 'your internal dialogues' in their book *Assertiveness at Work* (McGraw-Hill, 1986). In other words, what are you telling yourself when you act non-assertively or aggressively? Let's consider non-assertion first.

Fear of Displeasing Others. One reason why people act non-assertively is because they are afraid that they will experience disapproval. It may be disappointing, and sometimes disadvantageous, to be disapproved of by some significant person. (It is important to remember that you don't have to be assertive in any and every situation.) However, in most other cases where you would suffer no overt penalty or serious disadvantage, you will usually do better to act assertively.

When you act non-assertively to avoid displeasing someone important to you, you are usually going beyond defining that person's disapproval as merely a nuisance or an inconvenience. You define it as awful; you can't stand their disapproval or displeasure!

Changing Non-assertive Behaviour: A case study

Let's illustrate the beliefs behind non-assertion by taking this example of a woman who fears her friend's moodiness. Linda and Sharon shared a flat together and, since she had no car of her own, Sharon frequently borrowed Linda's car. The arrangement agreed between them was that Sharon could borrow the car provided that Linda did not need it herself, and provided that Sharon gave reasonable notice of her wish to use the car.

One evening Linda arrived home intending to drive over to visit her parents. As Linda was preparing to leave, she found a note left on the kitchen table which read, 'Linda, I've got a date tonight and have taken the car. Love, Sharon'.

Since Linda had received no advance notice that Sharon wanted to use the car that evening, she felt annoyed, and decided to take the matter up with Sharon. However, on second thoughts, Linda decided not to criticise Sharon's inconsiderate behaviour. The last time Linda had criticised Sharon for a fairly minor thing (using up the last of Linda's shampoo and failing to replace it), Sharon had sulked for days afterwards. Linda felt bad about that and so, not wishing to undergo another repetition of sulking, she decided to say nothing.

Linda's iBs. To maintain an attitude of non-assertion for fear of being disapproved of by her friend, Linda would be telling herself:

Behaviour	Intent	How You Feel
When you are *non-assertive*...	Your intent is to please, or avoid displeasing, the other person.	You tend to feel anxious, disappointed self-pitying, and sometimes angry with yourself later as a cover up for feeling 'weak'.
When you are *assertive*...	Your intent is to communicate with the other person in a way that promotes mutual respect.	You are self-accepting and accepting of the other person, and you feel confident.
When you are *aggressive*...	Your intent is to dominate or humiliate the other person.	You feel superior, or self-righteous. Perhaps later you experience guilt or embarrassment.

How Others Feel	Payoff	Outcome
Others tend to feel pity, disgust, or irritation when you approach them in such a self-effacing and self-deprecating manner.	You avoid conflict, confrontation, and the unpleasantness that often accompanies conflict and confrontation.	You don't usually get what you want. Frustration increases and your anger builds up.
Others tend to respect you and feel that you respect them.	You gain mutual respect. You create the possibility of a good relationship.	You frequently get what you want. Improved relationships can follow.
Others tend to feel angry and resentful.	You vent your anger and momentarily feel superior.	You may get what you want, often at others' expense. However, the resentment encourages others to 'get even' with you later.

'I must not displease her and risk losing her approval. I can't stand it when she feels hurt. It's all my fault if she feels hurt, and I'm a bad person for hurting her.'

The consequence of holding such a set of iBs would be a feeling of worthlessness, which in turn would discourage Linda from expressing what she really thinks and feels about the way she was treated.

Dispute. Imagine for a moment that you are in Linda's position. Now apply each of the three criteria for rationality to her beliefs:

Is this belief logical? You may not wish to displease your friend by criticising her, but it does not logically follow that you absolutely must not do so.

Is it realistic? No. In the first place, there is no law that says that anyone you criticise must not be displeased by it. Secondly, it is totally unrealistic to say that you can't stand it when Sharon feels hurt. She felt hurt when you criticised her before, yet here you are alive and well! Thirdly, is it really all your fault if Sharon feels hurt? You cannot take responsibility for another person's feelings.

Finally, you believe you are a bad person for hurting her. You infer that you hurt her, then condemn yourself for it. Even if you did, in fact, hurt her does a bad act make you a bad person? Humans are too complex ever to be given any kind of overall rating.

Does this belief help me achieve my goals? Since your belief discourages you from assertively confronting your friend, you are unlikely to achieve your goal of creating and maintaining a harmonious relationship based upon mutual respect and trust.

If you fear that someone whose behaviour you criticize will disapprove of you and that you cannot lose this person's love or approval, you are probably telling yourself something like. 'I must not say anything to hurt my friends because then they might withdraw and no longer love me, and that would be terrible!' So, to avoid that 'terrible' calamity, you act non-assertively and suffer the consequences of non-assertion.

Linda's rational alternative beliefs. 'If Sharon, or indeed any of my friends, feel hurt when I criticise their behaviour, that is too bad. I definitely would prefer to have my friends' approval, or at least avoid their disapproval, but I don't have to achieve either of these outcomes. If they withdraw or cease to show they care about me, that might disadvantage me, but it isn't terrible, and while I'll never like it, I can certainly bear it.'

Linda could then go on to explain to Sharon that she didn't hurt her; that she, Sharon, hurt herself because she mistakenly believed that Linda had deprecated her by her critical remarks when all that Linda had done was point out that some of Sharon's behaviour was unacceptable.

Once Linda had replaced her iBs with more rational or tough-minded convictions, she would be able to criticise unacceptable behaviour in an assertive manner, and reap the advantages of acting in such a manner.

Eliminating Aggressive Behaviour

Let's look at some of the reasons why people criticize others in an aggressive manner.

Whereas anger and hostility can arise when an individual perceives he has been frustrated or unfairly treated and believes he absolutely must not be, aggressive behaviour in interpersonal relations may be adopted as a means of defending oneself against feeling vulnerable and powerless in threatening situations.

In their book *The Assertive Option*, Patricia Jakubowski and Arthur J. Lange list no less than nine 'mind-sets' or beliefs that promote aggressive behaviour:

I *must* win in order to be OK.

If I don't come on strong, I won't be listened to.

The world is hostile, and I *must* be aggressive in order to make it.

To compromise is to lose.

I *must* make an impact.

I *must* get my way.

Aggression is the *only* way to get through to some people.

I *must* prove I'm right and they're wrong.

The world *must* be fair; it's intolerable when people mistreat me.

Have you noticed that all of the above beliefs have an unspoken 'tail' to them? In fact, all of them follow the 'I *must*' bit with an implicit conclusion of the form 'It would be *awful* if ...', or, 'I couldn't *bear* it if...', or, 'I'd be a worthless person if...', etc. All of these beliefs sound angry or hostile, but they are really all coverups for a low self-esteem. They all virtually mean 'I *must* succeed, or I'm no good!'

If you have reached the conclusion that non-assertion and aggression are not all that different from one another, you are correct: both stem from a feeling of being threatened by a situation or a person. The threat is not a physical one; the perceived threat is to the person's self-image, or self-esteem, the view that person has of himself or herself. If you feel threatened, you may behave non-assertively and thus avoid conflict; or you may behave aggressively to protect yourself from the inferred threat by hitting out. The old saying 'attack is the best form of defence' aptly makes this point.

Become Assertive, Not Aggressive

Becoming assertive therefore involves, first, identifying and challenging the iBs that support your aggressive tendencies, and secondly, replacing these with rational alternatives. Thus, if you previously believed, for example, 'I *must* prove I'm right and they are wrong', you need to replace that iB with:

'I'd definitely prefer to be proved right, but I don't have to. If it should turn out that I am wrong, I have learned something from my mistake. In any event, being proved right or wrong says nothing about my worth to myself. Since others have as much right to express their views as I have, I would be wise to respect their right, and thereby help to create a dialogue which is potentially of mutual benefit to us both.'

One final point. Becoming assertive in expressing constructive criticism requires not only that you acquire a rational philosophy, but also practice in using it. Expressing criticism in a healthy or constructive manner can be difficult, especially if you are dealing with Difficult People. A fear of being frustrated as you try to realise your objectives by the negative and uncooperative attitudes of Difficult People may lead to a lack of persistence on your part. Resist the temptation to give up and take it easy!

85

Get rid of your absolutistic 'shoulds', 'oughts', and 'musts'. These three words have a legitimate place in the language when used in a conditional, or non-absolute, sense — as, for example, when you say, 'I should have my video repaired if I want to record the film tonight', or, 'I must take my medicine if I want to get rid of this cough', and so on. These words are used in a non-imperative sense. They really mean, 'I *choose* to have my video repaired so that I can record the film', and 'I *choose* to take my medicine because I want to get rid of my cough.' It is when you place absolutistic demands upon yourself, other people, and the world, that you create needless problems for yourself and others. Absolutistic demands sabotage your goals of communicating healthy criticism in a constructive manner and block your hopes of improving mutual understanding.

Acquire instead a non-demanding philosophy such as REBT, and link it to the basic communicating skills you are learning in this chapter, and the further skills you will be shown in future chapters. If you learn and practise what we teach, you will find it much easier to cope when the going gets tough.

One final point: practise your new philosophy and the various skills you learn in a flexible manner. And remember, it's a lifetime project — *you don't just learn it and spontaneously do it by magic*. You must push yourself and practise for ever, probably for the rest of your life!

FOUR

Coping When Others Dislike and Hate You

*P*eople learn to be hostile, disparaging, and manipulative because it works for them. These people expect you to react in certain ways to their style, because in that way they win. If you allow yourself to be sucked into their expectations, you have not only let them get away, but you may often feel frustrated, helpless, and angry.

We will show you what you can do to eliminate unhelpful attitudes and replace them with rational, realistic alternatives.

How do you cope with people who show you that they actively dislike you, or even hate you? We're talking here of people who deliberately are rude, inconsiderate, unfair, manipulative, or even aggressive and irate; people who deliberately spread malicious rumours with the intention of getting you into trouble with somebody else — and often succeeding!

First, we will set the scene by explaining what it means to be dislikeable or hateable. Our aim is to provide you with several important insights into what is going on, both in your own mind and in the minds of others, when they dislike or hate you. These insights will enable you to cope constructively with being disliked or hated in a variety of situations.

Next, we will show you what not to do — how *not* to react when you are on the receiving end of someone's hostility or the object of someone's private vendetta. The usual reactions of people in these situations are anger, anxiety and guilt. We will show you why these negative, irrational emotions almost invariably block you from acting effectively in your own best interests, and we will show you what you can do to eliminate unhelpful attitudes and replace them with rational, realistic alternatives. You will then see how the leverage you gain from your more tough-minded approach will enable you to use your assertive communication skills with these people to defuse their nasty behaviour towards you.

What do 'Dislikeable' and 'Hateable' Really Mean? Some Insights.

To help us put this into perspective, we now introduce three Key insights.

Dislike Trait, Not the Person (Don't Judge the Person). Our first and most basic key point or key insight is this: you don't like somebody, or dislike or hate them, as a *person*. Why? Because liking or disliking, loving or hating, are evaluations of the person. You may evaluate a person's traits, characteristics, performances or abilities, but you cannot give someone an overall rating or assessment.

So what you really mean when you say 'I love you!' or 'I hate you!' is that you love or hate some characteristic, or trait that person seems to possess.

Since we cannot reasonably expect to change English usage overnight, people will continue to say 'I hate you', 'I dislike you', 'I love you', and so on. However, so long as you remember that all anyone can ever do is to like or dislike some *aspect* of you or your behaviour, you will avoid judging yourself, your total person, on the basis of how other people rate your traits or deeds. By the same token, you will wisely avoid rating others as persons on the same basis.

Accept Yourself: Don't let 'being disliked' affect you. People may dislike or hate you — that is to say, some aspect(s) of you — for all manner of reasons that simply reflect their own tastes, values, and personal prejudices. For example, they may dislike your accent, or the way you dress, or your skin colour, or religion. That is the way they are, and they are entitled to their tastes, values, and prejudices, in the same way that you are entitled to yours.

Avoid devaluing yourself. Sadly, some people deprecate themselves when they observe that others dislike or hate them. They easily convince themselves that, 'If people dislike or hate me, I'm basically a dislikeable person; therefore I'm no good!'

If ever you come to the conclusion that you are worthless then regardless of how you reached that conclusion, you have done yourself a great disservice. Let's show you why.

The irrationality of self-devaluation. As already pointed out, certain people may dislike or hate you for a variety of reasons. However, the most basic reason is that because you are a live human being with millions of traits, behaviours, and characteristics, and it is these, not you, that are potentially dislikeable or hateable.

Dispute. Now let's dispute the conclusion 'therefore I'm no good':

Is this conclusion logical? No, because you are arbitrarily equating being disliked or dislikeable with being no good. There is no necessary logical connection between being disliked, and having no value to yourself whatever. Better not define yourself at all, but simply accept yourself as having value to yourself because you are alive. In that way, you avoid any kind of self-rating whatsoever.

Is this conclusion realistic? Only if you believe in magic!

If you rate yourself as worthless merely on the basis of having some trait regarded as undesirable by others, you are making a magical jump from reality to unreality.

Does this conclusion help you achieve your goals? Obviously not. If you hate yourself when someone else dislikes or hates you, then you only add to your problems. In order to deal with the other person's feelings towards you, you first have to accept, not hate, yourself.

The Rational Alternative to Self-devaluation

If it is clear that some people definitely dislike or hate you, remember that the only thing they can dislike or hate about you is some observable feature or behaviour. Thus you could rationally believe the following:

> 'I definitely would prefer that others did not dislike or hate me because there are social and other disadvantages to being disliked. I'll never like being disliked or hated, but I can definitely stand it.
>
> 'Since I do not wish to appear arrogant or insensitive to the feelings of others with whom I work or socialise, I would be wise to try to discover what aspect of me is disliked. For example, if I am seen as overbearing, rude, or short-tempered, it might be in my best interests to try to eliminate or minimise these traits. I can always choose to accept myself unconditionally and resolve to be as happy as I can, with or without others' approval.'

With these more rational attitudes, you could try to establish a constructive dialogue with people who dislike or hate something about you, make whatever changes to your behaviour you deem desirable, and possibly establish a better relationship with them. However, also be prepared that you can't please everybody, and that some people, for their own reasons, may never accept you. Too bad — that's life, but you can still accept yourself unconditionally and get on with living your life as you see fit.

Analyse Your Actions. Key point 3 points out that while you may not have caused another person's disturbed negative feelings when you do them some harm, you have nevertheless contributed towards their distress through your actions. The essence of key point 3 is that while you do not cause other people to feel hateful or condemnatory of you as a person, when you harm them in some way, you do bear some responsibility for their feelings; and they are entitled to dislike being harmed by your wrongdoing, and to feel strongly motivated to secure compensation for the wrong they have suffered.

Now, having shown you what it means to be seen as dislikable or hateable, and why depreciating yourself on account of being disliked or dislikeable is totally unrealistic and unnecessary, we turn our attention to showing you how the REBT Insights and Disputing techniques can help you to target and eliminate three other irrational responses and disturbed negative reactions that you may experience when you become aware that some people dislike or hate you.

How to Cope Constructively with People Who Dislike or Hate You

Three disturbed negative emotions you might typically experience are anger, anxiety, and guilt. Our aim here is to show you how to deal constructively with these unhealthy reactions to being disliked or hated, and thereby contribute to improved relationships between yourself and others.

Never Get Angry with People who Dislike or Hate You: The case of Tom and Ronnie. Let's take one example. Tom was a young man who worked as a junior-level technician in a communications company that encouraged its employees to study in their own time for higher technical qualifications. Getting ahead in the company depended partly upon gaining certain technical certificates and partly on demonstrating an ability to do higher-grade work, including supervision of staff. So, taking a long-term view, Tom gave up certain pursuits to devote a good deal of his own time to obtaining these higher technical qualifications to strengthen his promotion claims.

Tom observed that some of his colleagues at work derided him for his attitude. They would play down the importance of technical education and try to convince him that 'certificates aren't everything', and that Tom was just wasting his time. Some of Tom's colleagues, resented him for allegedly 'trying to jump the promotion queue by impressing people with certificates'.

A sad day! The day arrived when Tom was due to sit his 'finals'. It was a three-hour evening exam, and after finishing work Tom had an hour or so to 'kill' before the examination. Bob, a cleaner at work, with whom Tom did not have much in common, but who had always been very nice to his face, approached Tom and suggested that since he had some time to pass why not have a drink together?

Soon Tom found himself in a pub with Bob, who seemed to be a much friendlier person than Tom had previously thought. Bob insisted on paying and chatted animatedly about things that interested Tom. Suddenly Tom remembered the time! Too late! While Tom and

Bob had been drinking and chatting, the time had seemingly passed more quickly than either of them had realised. Bob was very apologetic and tried to confort Tom for getting late for exam.

Feeling really annoyed with himself for having so carelessly miffed his chance, Tom acquiesced and had another round of drinks with Bob. Then, next day, as he thought about what had happened the previous evening, Tom realised that he'd been set up! Tom recalled that Bob was a close friend of another guy called Ronnie, who seemed to resent Tom, and who fancied himself for the senior tech position in the company in spite of his failure to obtain the higher qualifications. Tom figured that Ronnie had put his pal up to it. Tom knew that he had a good chance of gaining the top technical qualifications if he had passed that exam, and he also knew that he had never had a drink with Ronnie's pal before. As Tom recalled later, 'So why last night, of all nights, did Bob take me out for a drink? A coincidence? Not likely!' So Tom lost a whole year's work, and would have to wait another year before he could have another crack at the exam, while Ronnie would get a shot at the soon-to-become-vacant senior tech job coming up and pondered ways of getting even with him.

Why Tom made Himself Angry at his Workmates. Tom felt angry and hurt at the way he considered he had been treated by his workmates, especially Ronnie. He inferred that he had been the victim of a dirty tricks campaign, and that he had done nothing to deserve such treatment. Tom suspected, but could not prove, that Ronnie had set him up and pondered ways of getting even with him.

If you look back at how Tom reacted to these events, you will see that he considered he had been unfairly treated and that he didn't think he deserved to be. He felt that his personal rules of behaviour had been violated (see box below). When you make yourself angry when other people frustrate you, by transgressing your personal rules of behaviour, it is because you have a philosophy of LFT and/or a set of beliefs centred on lowered self-esteem. Now, in view of what we know of Tom's reactions, both immediately, and the day after his unfortunate experience, we have evidence that frustration over the failure of the staff to treat Tom with the level of consideration he demanded, was the source of his anger. Tom certainly did not lack self-esteem, since he attached great importance to taking exams and getting ahead on technical merit. Therefore category (d) would appear to offer the more appropriate framework in which to discuss Tom's anger.

Look for Your Inferences

When you are angry at other people, the inferences you make about the events that triggered your anger involve four major themes:

a. situtations where other people frustrate or block you in the pursuit of your goals;

b. situations where other people directly attack you or what you value;

c. situations where you perceive yourself or your values threatened by other people;

d. situations where other people transgress your personal rules of behaviour.

The iBs behind Tom's anger. To Tom, life would be grim, almost intolerable, if he failed to rise above the junior technician ranks and had to spend the rest of his working life doing repetitive low-level technical work, and he was sure he could do better than that.

Tom's anger springs from his demand that he must be treated with a degree of consideration in the pursuit of his goals. Tom's feeling of 'hurt' springs from his 'poor me' attitude, which is implied in the conclusions that follow from his primary demand; these conclusions are:

- 'It's terrible that some of my colleagues treat me in a manner I do not deserve.'

- 'I can't stand to be treated in this way because of the hard life I'd be faced with if I fail to pass my exams and remain at my present job level.'

- 'They are rotten people for treating me this way.'

As you can see, the real issue turns out to be Tom's rule, *his* expectation, that his colleagues treat him with justice, fairness and consideration. Tom's anger arises because he believes that his colleagues are transgressing his rule.

Dispute. Now let's see why Tom's beliefs are irrational.

'Since I treat my colleagues with consideration, they must reciprocate. I don't deserve to be blocked from achieving my occupational objectives, and I must not get what I don't deserve.'

Is this belief logical? Does it logically follow that because Tom treats his colleagues with consideration therefore his colleagues must reciprocate? Obviously not.

97

Whatever we might desire, there is never any logical reason why we must have our desire fulfilled.

Is it realistic? Again, the answer is no. Whenever you demand that people accede to your wishes, and if they fail to do so, your 'must' obviously doesn't apply. Is there was some law that said that Tom's considerate behaviour towards his colleagues must always be reciprocated.

Likewise, if you get the kind of treatment you think you don't deserve, there is no reason why the world must oblige you by arranging that you never get the kind of behaviour that you think you don't deserve.

Does this belief help Tom achieve his goals? It is most unlikely! People may or may not treat you in the way you want, but once you believe that others *must* treat you in a certain way, you will find that they are unlikely to oblige you. You may win respect and consideration from others, but you can hardly demand it.

Tom's sulking behaviour, that stemmed from his belief that he must be respected, would be more likely to lower the amount of respect accorded to him by his colleagues.

Control Your Anger (With People Who Dislike You). Assuming for the moment that Tom's perceptions of his colleagues' attitudes towards him were accurate, what could Tom more rationally believe about his situation?

'Since I treat my colleagues with consideration, I would definitely prefer that they reciprocate, but they don't have to. I have my values and they are equally entitled to theirs. I can still pursue my occupational goals whether or not my colleagues share my views.

'I won't ever enjoy being treated with less consideration than I would like, but I can obviously stand it.

I alone am responsible for allowing myself to be sidetracked, and I feel annoyed for having possibly lost valuable time as a result. There is no sense in blaming someone else for my mistake.'

With these rBs, Tom would feel annoyed at losing a year of his time, but he would also feel determined to steam ahead with studies in the hope of making up for the opportunity lost through his own negligence. These rBs would enable Tom to view his situation without anger, but instead with healthy annoyance.

Two key advantages of holding rBs are that once you make them an integral part of your psychological make-up, you gain control over your own emotions and the ability to take charge of your life.

Don't Feel Anxious: Counter attack your anxiety (About people who dislike you)

Another way in which you feel needlessly upset when others dislike or hate you is when you get anxious about some event that might happen, and to which you feel powerless to make any constructive response.

John had been engaged to Jane for about a year when he came to the conclusion that they were not really well suited and as a result John had broken off the engagement. Although Jane was upset for a time, she soon regained her equilibrium when she too realised that breaking off had been in their best interests.

Unfortunately, Jane's maiden aunt, Bernadette, took a different view. She was furious with John, told him she hated him for 'treating her niece in such a rotten manner', and threatened to expose him 'for the rogue that he was'.

John was not afraid of any physical harm, but he was aware of the damage to his reputation that Bernadette could cause. Jane's aunt was well known in the community, and was friendly with many influential people. John began to feel anxious that sooner or later he would bump into Bernadette in public. He knew that she would not lose an opportunity like that to tell him off in front of everyone.

In order to avoid a confrontation John began to spend more time indoors. He hated being stuck indoors but the thought of meeting Bernadette in public terrified him. Then one day his worst fears were realised. John was standing in a bank queue waiting to cash a cheque when Bernadette spotted him. 'So there you are, you two-timing little cheat! You've got some nerve showing your face here after what you did to my poor niece!' bawled Bernadette in a loud voice. 'You broke that poor girl's heart and I hope you rot in hell!'

Noticing that some customers looked embarrassed and that some were giggling over Bernadette's outburst, John, looking white as a sheet, ran out of the bank.

Now John's anxiety developed rapidly. He worried incessantly about the 'horror' of getting involved in yet another public encounter with Bernadette, and spent still more time indoors.

Put yourself in John's place for a moment. It's a fact that worry can develop into a very painful condition. If you exaggerate the assumed catastrophic quality of the unpleasant events you fear might happen, worrying about them only makes you feel worse.

100

Apart from the possibility of physical harm or being literally starved what can you ever really fear? You usually do have more control over the circumstances of your life than you think, and you can change various aspects if you learn to think rationally and stop panicking. Now, let's see what John could do to eliminate his anxiety about the situation he found himself in.

What really caused John's anxiety? It wasn't the threat of being branded as an insensitive cad that really upset John — it was what John was telling himself about this threat.

> 'This threat absolutely must not occur and it would be terrible if it did.'

So long as you maintain the iBs that create anxiety, your attempts to cope with the anxiety-provoking situation are likely to be ineffective at best, or unhealthy at worst.

How John counter-attacked his anxiety. First, John identified and challenged his belief about the assumed 'awfulness' of the threat of being slandered in public. This belief was: 'This threat absolutely must not occur and it would be terrible if it did.'

Is this belief logical? John fervently wished that the threat of being branded a cheat should not materialise. We may wish for all sorts of things, but there is no logical necessity that our wishes must be granted.

Is it realistic? If it was realistic, we would merely have to wave a magic wand, intone the words 'This must not happen!' and it wouldn't!

John's conclusion that it would be terrible if the threat of being 'humiliated' in public did actually occur is a fine example of gross exaggeration. To lose one's reputation may be hard, and we may feel deprived, but realistically speaking, it is hardly terrible.

Does this belief help John achieve his goals? The answer is very probably no. If we try to deal with a situation while holding beliefs about it that are illogical and unrealistic, we are unlikely to take the right kind of constructive actions to improve matters and more likely take actions that are be counter-productive.

The Rational Alternative to Anxiety. Once John had convinced himself that anxiety was unnecessary and needlessly getting in the way of taking constructive action, he could replace the iBs that created his anxiety with more rational convictions.

'I definitely would prefer that this threat of Bernadette's to destroy my reputation did not occur. If she persists in slandering me, I will serve a writ on her for defamation of character.'

With these beliefs, John would feel concern at the possible damage to his reputation, but he would not be utterly afraid of it happening. In addition to attacking his irrational fears verbally, he could act actively by pushing himself to go out and deliberately confront Bernadette, that he wasn't afraid of her and that nothing terrible happens to him when he does confront her.

Realise that most anxieties relate to some dire fear of disapproval, but if you strongly challenge and fight this fear by showing yourself that disapproval or loss of reputation may bring disadvantages, or inconvenience, you will realise that any 'horrors' exist only in your imaginative ability to define them as such.

Don't Feel Guilty or Blame Yourself if People Dislike You

In this section we show you healthy ways of responding to someone's scorn and hate when you are guilty of needlessly and wilfully harming them.

What does 'Feeling Guilty' Really Mean? Let's make one thing clear at the start. If you've deliberately committed an immoral, illegal, or anti-social act and have wilfully harmed somebody as a result, you are guilty of a bad act or misdeed or an offence. Does that mean that you must also *feel* guilty? Not necessarily! You preferably should only feel guilty in the sense of firmy resolving to avoid committing offence again, and resolving to make restitution to the person you gratuitously injured. Guilt represents feelings of inadequacy and self-hatred. Let's take a closer look at what is implied by a sense of guilt, or self-blame.

What Creates a Feeling of Guilt? A feeling of guilt occurs when you firmly convince yourself of the following:

> 'I have committed a wrong act and am responsible for doing it. Therefore I am a rotten person for having done this wrong deed.'

Does that sound rational to you? Let's see.

Is this belief logical? Essentially this belief states: 'I'm responsible for doing a wrong thing, therefore I'm worthless.' There is no logical connection between 'I've done a wrong thing' and the conclusion 'therefore I'm worthless.' The conclusion is nothing more than how one feels about having done the wrong deed in question. *Is it realistic?* The first part is realistic. 'I have committed a wrong act and am responsible for doing it'. That can be objectively confirmed and verified. However, is the second part — 'therefore I am a rotten person' — a factual statement?

As we have argued previously, labelling an entire person as rotten — or, for that matter, as good — cannot be logically validated. All we have in this world are people with good and bad traits. You may find that hard to swallow, but once you see it clearly, you will tend to see yourself and others as fallible individuals with good and bad traits, but never as rotten individuals.

Does this belief help me reach my goals? Not unless your goal is to become a miserable, self-hating individual! The real question that concerns you is acknowledging, 'I have done a wrong act. Now, how can I learn to make sure that I don't repeat it in future?' However, to acknowledge that honestly, necessitates abandoning your guilt-creating beliefs and replacing them with more rational convictions.

The Rational Alternative to Guilt. The rational alternative to guilt is regret or remorse. You feel badly about your wrong act, but not about yourself. Thus you could believe:

> 'I admit that I committed a wrong act; I am responsible for it and I regret it. However, I am not a rotten person deserving of punishment, but a fallible human who will sometimes act badly. Now let me see how I can make amends for the harm I have caused and, more importantly, see how I can stop myself from harming someone again in the future.'

With this more rational, healthier attitude, you will be motivated to focus on how you do not repeat your wrong behaviour in future, instead of dwelling on how to punish yourself for your past wrongdoing. In this way, you will help yourself to learn to behave less immorally.

The iBs of People who Dislike or Hate You

Now, why will it help you to understand the iBs of others?

You may safely assume that when others double-cross you, or behave towards you in manipulative, aggressive, resentful, or dishonest ways, the behaviour of these people springs from either ignorance, stupidity, or emotional disturbance. Once you understand why people act towards you in the way they do, you can sometimes help them to act more constructively. Even if you cannot achieve such a positive outcome, you may at least succeed in diminishing unnecessary strife and emotional disturbances between you and your associates.

When Someone Feels Threatened by You

When someone feels threatened by you, one common reason is that they believe that they *must* get what they want and see you as a threat to reaching their goal. In the case of Tom that we discussed in a previous section, Tom suspected that his colleague, Ronnie, had engineered a plot to make him miss his exam in order to promote Ronnie's own chances of winning the senior tech job in the company. To Ronnie, failure to win promotion to the senior tech position would lower his reputation among his colleagues, and seriously damage his self-esteem.

Ronnie's iB about this was:

'I must, absolutely must, win promotion to the senior supervisory position in this company. If I fail, that would prove I'm no good.'

By imposing this demand upon himself, Ronnie made himself anxious over the possibility that he might fail to clinch the promotion. To improve his own chances, therefore, Ronnie used unfair tactics to prevent his rival from being offered the senior tech job.

You will recognise Ronnie's iB as a variant of Major Irrational Belief No. 1 which can be found on page 35.

Compare Major Irrational Belief No. 1 with Ronnie's variant or derivative:

'I must win promotion to the senior supervisory position in this company. If I fail, that would prove I'm no good.'

Ronnie's rational alternative beliefs. 'I strongly prefer to win promotion to the senior tech supervisory position, but I don't absolutely have to. If I fail, that will be disappointing, but not a disaster. If I fail, all that it will prove is that I failed on this particular occasion. One failure doesn't make me a total failure. I can always try again, and by working to improve my chances I may be successful in winning promotion in future.'

With these rational convictions, Ronnie would be more interested in discovering what he could do to improve his own promotion rating rather than trying to spoil that of his rival.

How their rBs can help Tom and Ronnie to cope with their rivalry in a mutually helpful manner. The advantages that both Tom and Ronnie obtain by replacing their iBs with rBs about themselves and their work are:

- Their respective feelings of angry hurt and self-deprecation are replaced by the more helpful feelings of annoyance and regret. Tom will no longer damn his colleagues for not giving him the measure of respect he previously demanded of them. He will accept them as they are, and devote himself to working towards his own goals without animosity to others who do not share his views.

- Ronnie will no longer believe that he absolutely must succeed in winning promotion. Instead he will continue to demonstrate his determination to succeed through the quality of his work, rather than by devising schemes to derail the chances of his rivals.

- Both Tom and Ronnie are likely to achieve better cooperation once they abandon their iBs and no longer see one another as adversaries, but instead as friendly rivals.

The point being made here is that in all walks of life we are bound to meet people who dislike or hate something about us. However, that does not mean that we cannot possibly get along. You don't necessarily have to like someone, or share their views and values, to get along with them. Provided you give up your demands on others and make allowances for their iBs and demands upon you, a reasonable level of co-operation can be achieved in most instances.

Understanding the iBs of others when you act badly towards them. What we have said about combating your own irrational guilt-producing beliefs applies equally to the beliefs of other people who condemn you for acting wrongly. They may dislike you for your misdeeds, but, realistically speaking, they can only judge your deeds, not you, the person. You can show your detractors that you understand how they feel, and even indicate that if you saw yourself as others saw you, you could even agree with them: 'If I were in your shoes I'd dislike me too!' Make allowances for the way others perceive you and your errors, and strive to accept them as you would like them to accept you.

Communicating More Effectively with People who Dislike or Hate You

As we have seen, people may dislike or hate you for all sorts of reasons. You may have been guilty of some wrong-doing. Some people may be prejudiced against you because of your colour or ethnic origin, or your nationality, or they may just dislike some physical or personality trait you possess.

The most important thing to remember is not to create a problem about the problem by getting yourself all 'stewed up' over the fact of being disliked. You would prefer that they were not so prejudiced, but if they are, they are, and that's their problem. Why make it your problem as well?

People learn to be hostile, disparaging, and manipulative because it works for them, as they have found that behaving in these ways programmes others to react in certain set typical ways. These people expect you to react in certain ways to their style, because in that way they win. If you allow yourself to be sucked into their expectations, that helps to maintain their ineffective behaviour; you have not only let them get away with it but you will often feel frustrated, helpless, and angry. At work, this can be undermining and demotivating for those who are on the receiving end of such tactics, leading to loss of efficiency and productivity. At home, similar communication tactics cause personal and family relationships to suffer, sometimes to the point of breakdown.

We will focus now on some examples of communication styles that express the private agendas of the initiators rather than promote understanding and cooperation among those to whom the communications are addressed.

Stand up to Hostile and Aggressive People

You are sitting at your desk when suddenly your boss comes charging in. Standing over you in a very intimidating manner, he throws your carefully prepared development plan on to your desk and yells, 'This development plan of yours is the stupidest thing I've ever read.' Then turning to face the rest of the office staff, he launches into a detailed and unrelenting attack on your plan. When he finally runs out of steam he stomps off, leaving you fuming with rage and totally demoralised.

Your reaction is understandable, but it robs you of the ability to deal coolly and competently with the situation. If you fight back and shout him down, where will that get you? Probably the door marked EXIT. On the other hand, if you let yourself be steamrollered into the ground, you will be seen as weak and unsure.

Bosses like that have a strong need to prove to themselves and to others that their view of things is right. 'I absolutely must be right, and seen to be right!' is their basic irrational conviction. Making others look weak or stupid makes this type of boss feel superior and important. They are angry with, and feel justified in humiliating, those subordinates who do not do what they should. Then they devalue you when you respond in the weak and ineffectual manner they expect of you.

How to cope with a bullying boss. Your object is not to change your boss, but cope with him. Don't blame him for being the way he is. He may have a problem, but he acts the way he does because he has got away with it in the past. Convince yourself that it is too bad that your boss is the way he is, but that's all it is — too bad. It is not catastrophic.

The purpose of coping is to help you to avoid feeling helpless and frustrated. It also aims to establish some kind of rational discussion between you and your boss. You achieve it by applying the principle of standing up to your boss without fighting him.

Step 1. Stand up to him. Look him straight in the eye and, in a tone of voice that matches his own voice in intensity, say (calling him by his name): 'Mr Jones! I'm afraid I disagree with you! In my judgement I think you may have overlooked certain significant facts. But tell me more about what's bothering you about my plan.'

The chances are your boss will have interrupted you after your first few words. He knows what you are going to say, he expects excuses to start coming, and why should he waste his time listening to them? So, still looking him straight in the eye, you say:

Step 2. 'Mr Jones, you interrupted me!' Not, 'Don't interrupt me!' These three words sound like fighting words, and fighting is the very thing you do not want to get into.

Step 3. Return to you conversation, and make your points. Use 'I' language, Don't say, 'You're wrong about such-and-such.' Say things like, 'I know you're the boss and what you say goes, but in my opinion ...'

Expect to be interrupted again, and repeat your earlier words:

Step 4. 'Mr Jones, you interrupted me!' 'You interrupted me *again*!' Once more, that sounds too much like fighting talk. You are trying to defuse his hostility and turn a confrontation into a problem-solving discussion.

Step 5. Resume the conversation. Once he has calmed down enough, you will notice a quite remarkable change. Because he never really did see you before as you are now. If you have successfully stood up to your boss without him feeling personally defeated, you may find him making friendly overtures. Having been unable to overwhelm you, he may now see you as worthy of respect; or he may feel a need for acceptance, which is expressed by offering friendship.

Confront the Passive-aggressive Person who Hates You

When someone hates you, she/he may consider it unwise or inexpedient, due to social or other constraints, to attack in an openly aggressive manner. What can happen is that the person who hates you will find some relatively safe way of harming you or your interests in a manner that makes it virtually impossible for the aggressor to be identified.

The passive-aggressive person typically uses indirect and dishonest methods to achieve a desired goal. For example, one person in a relationship may use manipulative strategies to get the other person to agree to something the first person wants by playing on the victim's compassion, fear, or guilt.

Confronting the Problem. First, bring the problem out into the open. You may, for example, have a disgruntled subordinate who feels you haven't given him a fair deal. Maybe you didn't really listen to his legitimate complaints or take heed of his suggestions for constructive changes to certain operating procedures. Or perhaps your secretary, despite her continuous complaints of sexual harassment in the office, feels angry with you, and increasingly frustrated and demoralised over the fact that you are still doing nothing about it. Once you have identified the source of the conflict. You could act as follows:

Step 1. Invite the person to sit down with you to discuss matters of mutual concern. Explain that your object is to invite the person to bring out anything that may be troubling him or her, so that you can work out what can be done to put matters right.

Step 2. Without adopting a threatening or overbearing manner, set the tone of the discussion by saying something like:

'What would you most like to talk about right now', or,

'What specifically is bothering you?' or,

'What specifically do you want done, or have changed, that is a problem for you?'

112

Step 3. Indicate through your attitude that you accept that the person has a grievance, and that your main desire is to get at the facts and to put the matter right.

Step 4. Think about the kind of person you are dealing with; ask yourself what his or her likely motivations are, and what coping steps might be needed. Thus, throughout the encounter, employ active listening; frequently paraphrase what the other person is saying so that she/he feels understood. 'So, am I understanding you correctly if I say that you feel upset over the fact that the complaint you made to me was just ignored?'

Step 5. When you and the person opposite have reached a mutually agreed understanding of what the problem is, the way is then open for you both to reach some agreement, on what specific action will be taken to resolve the problem.

Role-playing can be useful in coaching people how to deal successfully in real-life situations with others who may be difficult to deal with. If you use friends or colleagues to role-play various attitudes, make sure that at least one of you is conversant with the basics of assertion and with REBT. Remember, too, that role-playing assertive responses, don't necessarily guarantee that you will be successful in real life. There are no guarantees! No rules saying you *have* to get what you want. Show yourself, through using the REBT insights you've gained, that none of the communication skills you are learning *have* to work. There are no '*have to's* in the universe.

When Others Dislike you Because of their Personality Disorder

The worst thing you can do is to get angry back at

such people. When others hate you, it is sometimes because of a personality disorder over which they may have little or no control. Make allowances for their personality disorder, and try to accept them with their handicap. Be wary, be firm, but be fair. It's healthy to feel displeased and frustrated when others dislike or hate you, rather than trying to be calm, disinterested, or disposed to turn the other cheek. Understanding and empathizing with those who dislike or hate you when you are not disturbed yourself, will pay dividends through enabling you to cope better with such people than if you return hatred with hatred, or anger with anger.

We are all fallible humans, mistake-making animals. However, we also have that unique human ability to think rationally about ourselves and the world, to learn from experience, to exercise judgement and restraint and hopefully, to make fewer mistakes in the future. Let's use that ability!

FIVE

Expressing Healthy Disapproval and Annoyance

There are considerable advantages to be gained from being able to express disapproval or annoyance of others' poor behaviour in an appropriately healthy or assertive manner.

Conversely, you put yourself at a disadvantage if you fail to express healthy disapproval to someone who treats you badly, either because you overreact, or because you fail to show any reaction at all.

*W*hy are we writing a chapter on learning how to express healthy disapproval and annoyance when others treat you, or your loved ones, in unfair or inconsiderate ways?

Advantages of Expressing Disapproval in a Healthy Way

Firstly, there are considerable advantages to be gained from being able to express disapproval or annoyance of others' poor behaviour in an appropriately healthy or assertive manner.

Secondly, when someone treats you or your loved ones in inconsiderate or unfair ways, your ability to take a view of that person's behaviour and to communicate it in a manner likely to elicit an apology, is a skill that few of us are born with. It's a skill we have to learn.

Thirdly, you may put yourself at a disadvantage if you fail to express healthy disapproval to someone who treats you badly, either because you overreact, or because you fail to show any reaction at all.

Successful Expression of a Healthy Disapproval: Some insights

We will now look at the main reasons why some people fail to express disapproval and annoyance in an appropriately healthy and assertive manner, when they are treated unfairly or inconsiderately by others.

1. Distinguish Annoyance from Anger

Have you ever experienced a strong sense of righteous anger over someone's 'outrageous' behaviour? You are not alone! Denunciation fuelled by a strong sense of moral indignation over some person's attitude or behaviour comes easily to many — perhaps most — of us, since expressing anger often makes you feel good.

What have you achieved, though? The person who has violated your sense of right and wrong, or upset your notion of fair play, may be contrite and resolve not to behave like that again. But don't bank on it! Chances are that most adults will resent being told off, and will close off communication.

Angry denunciation of people is unlikely to persuade them to apologize, and still less to make amends for their poor behaviour. Does this mean, then, that you just have to squelch your angry feelings, deny and repress them? Not at all. Your anger hasn't disappeared just because you've been repressing it. It's there alright, ready to boil over at the slightest thing. You become overly critical of people and things you disapprove of.

'But look here!' some of you will exclaim at this point. 'On the one hand, you advise us not to sit on our anger because of the bad physiological effects it could have on our health. On the other hand, you're telling us that if we express our anger, we make matters even worse for ourselves. So, just what are we expected to do with our anger?'

The answer is to *undercut* your anger. Look behind it and seek out the iBs that created it in the first place, and uproot them. Then replace these iBs with rational alternative beliefs that will enable you to express

118

disapproval in a healthy and appropriately assertive manner. You will feel annoyed or displeased when others treat you unfairly, but you won't feel angry. You won't lose your 'cool'.

'But isn't annoyance much the same feeling as anger?' You may ask. 'Isn't annoyance just a milder or less severe form of anger?' Our answer is 'Definitely not!' You feel as you think. Therefore if you wish to change a feeling — anger, for example — you have to identify and change the ideas, or beliefs that lie behind the feeling of anger, and replace them with more rational convictions.

Beliefs that Make you Angry. Suppose someone has treated you very unfairly and you decide to express your disapproval. For example, your boss has forgotten how you gave up your lunch break recently to help him get some urgent work done, and when you asked him for the time off in lieu he had promised, he refused on the grounds that he was short-staffed. On the same day, you discover that a colleague has been granted leave to visit a sick relative in hospital.

Feeling angry, you demand to see your boss and accuse him of favouritism. Your boss reacts angrily, tells you it is none of your business whom he decides to give time off to, and orders you back to your desk.

Inwardly seething, you are telling yourself, 'He absolutely has to be fair to me! He is a rotten person for reneging on his promise to let me have time off. Before you can handle this situation in a manner more likely to help you achieve an acceptable outcome, you need to rid yourself of your anger.

Dispute. Let's take the first part of the belief: 'He absolutely has to be fair to me!'

Is this belief logical? Here you are really saying that because you want your boss to be fair to you, therefore he absolutely has to. Does it logically follow that your wish must be granted? Obviously not!

Is it realistic? If it was realistic, wouldn't whatever you wished for automatically be granted? But since you don't control the universe, there is no guarantee that anything you want has to be granted.

Moreover, your assertion that your boss is a rotten person for giving someone else time off, when it was allegedly your turn to take time off, is another arbitrary value judgement that reflects your opinion, but that cannot be objectively proved.

Does this belief help you achieve your goals? It's unlikely! Why? Well, suppose that you confront your boss and that you say to him, 'Look here! I demand that you treat me fairly at all times, and if you don't, you are a rotten person deserving of punishment!' How could you expect him to react? We would wager that even the most accommodating of bosses would find your attitude unreasonable to say the least, while others less accommodating would point you to the way out.

Annoyance: The rational alternative to anger. Annoyance is not simply a milder kind of anger, but springs from very different beliefs. The physical effects of anger and annoyance are also very different. When you are angry — really enraged — your adrenaline level rises abruptly. Your heart beats faster: you tense up and feel ready to strike out. People can tell you are angry just by looking at you.

By contrast, when you feel annoyed, even intensely annoyed, you can usually conceal it. And annoyance, in all probability, doesn't produce those dangerous physiological side effects that are caused by anger. So, how do you get to annoyance, rather than anger, when somebody treats you unfairly or inconsiderately, and you decide to do something about it?

The rational alternative. Taking the example used you could take the following rational approach:

> 'My boss has treated me unfairly by refusing me time off that I was due. I would find it highly preferable if he treated me fairly and kept his word. But I can see no reason why he must treat me fairly. He is not a rotten person for having treated me unfairly, but a fallible human who occasionally does wrong things.'

If you were to stick completely with that rB, you would merely feel sorry, displeased, or annoyed with the poor treatment you had received, but you would not feel angry. You could (calmly) explain to your boss why you felt you had been treated unfairly in view of the extra time of your own you had given him when he asked for it, and you could ask him to suggest a time when you could be absent that would be acceptable to both of you.

If you find yourself being treated unfairly or inconsiderately, getting angry with the offending person is unlikely to help you express your disapproval, in a way that will encourage that person to admit that his behaviour was unfair, or to change it. Your wisest option, therefore, when you feel your anger rising, is to replace your anger-creating philosophy with more rational ideas. You will then enable yourself to undercut and change your previous counter-productive responses to your anger.

2. Distinguish the Individual from his Behaviour

'You are not the same as your traits!' You will have already come across this statement and we hope, have understood and appreciated its truth. We draw attention to it again here for two reasons.

First, most people have pronounced self-denigrating tendencies. Bearing that in mind, if you attempt to express your disapproval of some aspect of a person's behaviour, or of their personality, then unless you are careful in your choice of words, you may find that they carry the implications of your remarks further than you intended. Then, in an attempt to ward off feelings of guilt or self-recrimination, they try to get back at you for 'attacking' them. Since that is not the response you were aiming for, your manner of expressing disapproval would have been counter-productive.

Our second reason for focusing attention on the importance of distinguishing a person's traits from the total person is that when one is angry, one easily tends to merge the 'disapproved of' action or behaviour with the total person. As a result, we end up by equating the person's poor behaviour with the entire person. When that happens, this one-sided and negative evaluation of the person alienates that individual, who is likely to respond in a defensive manner to protect his or her self-image. This, in turn, negates the likelihood of achieving a constructive resolution to the problem.

Learning to Accept Yourself and Others. The main point we wish to make here is that you can accept yourself and others while not accepting certain behaviour. When someone performs a good act we frequently hear that individual referred to as 'a good person'. The opposite also holds true. She/he then becomes 'a bad person'. There are no totally 'good' or 'bad' people so far as we know.

We have already seen that when you put someone down for not living up to your expectations, anger results. That is why it is most important that you work at eliminating the idea that someone is a rotten person for having certain traits or behaving in certain ways that you disapprove of. Once you make progress in this area, you can then try to find practical solutions or negotiate acceptable compromises. While you are about it, learning to accept yourself when your own behaviour falls short of your own standards is as important as learning to accept others. When you put yourself down as a total person, guilt and/or depression result. This leads us naturally on to discussing the third main block to expressing healthy disapproval or annoyance.

3. You don't Always have to be Nice

Some people are very loath to express disapproval or annoyance over the way they are being treated, even when they would be quite justified in doing so. The idea that one must always be polite to others at least in public, is one of these socio-cultural messages to which many of us have been exposed, during our impressionable years.

On one level, most people would agree that it is nonsense to hold that we have to be nice to people all the time. However, on another (and deeper) level, they feel anxious about speaking up and expressing their disapproval or annoyance to someone, even when speaking up would clearly be justified.

What are You Really Afraid of? The only thing you're probably afraid of is that you may sound stupid to those within earshot, and they are going to think badly of you. You are afraid others are going to think, 'Hey, listen to this! Who does he or she think she is, talking like that? God?' You are then going to believe that you're no good, because you have the belief, 'You have to be nice to people, and nice people like you don't make a fuss and get thought of badly.'

Now hold on a minute! The goal of asserting yourself is not to put the other person down or to get what you want at all costs — that is being aggressive. Being assertive simply means expressing your opinions, needs, and desires openly and honestly while respecting the right of the other person to do the same. What's wrong about that?

Now, assuming that your goal is to express healthy disapproval or annoyance without putting yourself down for doing so, how would you go about it? The answer is: tackle the iB that says if someone calls you unflattering names when you express disapproval of their behaviour, you have to take their words to heart and consider yourself a worm or a louse for speaking out. By this stage in your reading, you will need no reminding that you don't *have* to do anything.

Consequently, we shall not waste time disputing the idea that 'you have to be nice to people'. It is the conclusion you tend to draw from that idea that causes you to feel bad about yourself.

Does it logically follow that you are a louse because someone says you are? Obviously not! Being defined as this or that is nothing more than someone's arbitrary definition.

Is the belief realistic? In no way! Imagine if someone called you a millionaire. Would being called a millionaire suddenly transform you into a millionaire? Some hope! So, by the same token, if somebody calls you 'bossy' or 'pushy' etc., that may be just their opinion. You can be called all sorts of things, but you don't have to take the words seriously.

Does this belief help you achieve your goals? Not unless you enjoy putting yourself down! The chances are that when people notice you taking their criticisms or innuendos to heart, they will tend to capitalize on the situation by prodding at you with their barbed remarks when you speak out, and your chances of getting them to stop or change their treatment of you will fade.

Hold your Head up High! The Rational Alternative to Putting yourself Down. If you want to be treated with respect and consideration and to express your views openly and honestly in appropriate circumstances without feeling anxious or embarrassed, you can do so by giving up those self-deprecating beliefs that have held you down in the past.

Once you have convinced yourself that those previous iBs are only giving you a false image and doing you no good whatsoever, you will find yourself ready to consider an alternative, more rational, and positively helpful way of looking at yourself in relation to other people.

'While I don't like being called uncomplimentary names when I express my disapproval of someone's unfair treatment of me or my loved ones, there is no reason why others must not say uncomplimentary things about me. I have a right, to express my views about the way I am treated, and if others dislike it when I speak up and express my disapproval or annoyance, that is their problem. It doesn't mean I have to agree with them. If I have a point to make, I will make it clearly and firmly and without apology, while maintaining the right of my detractors to express their opinions.

If you stay with that more rational way of viewing your situation, you will not upset yourself when others try to ignore or play down your expression of disapproval by calling you names in the hope of pressing your shame buttons. With a rational philosophy you undercut the iBs that formerly created your shame and anxiety, and being called names will consequently no longer be a problem for you.

The Pros and Cons of Assertively Communicating Healthy Disapproval

Let's assume that you are now ready to deal appropriately with people who treat you unfairly or inconsiderately. While there are advantages to being able to communicate disapproval and annoyance in an assertive manner, there are also a few disadvantages you may wish to consider. To remind ourselves of what we mean by 'communicating healthy disapproval and annoyance assertively', and how assertive communication differs in certain important respects from both aggressive and non-assertive communication see pages 76-77.

In assertion you try to get what you want and avoid what you don't want. However, you accept that your wishes don't have to be acceded to. When you demand that others accede to your wishes you add a hostile component to your feelings and behaviour, based on

126

the iB that you must get what you want and that others have no right to block you.

Assertive behaviour enables you to achieve your goals without infringing the rights of others to go for what they want. Assertive behaviour leads to the development of mutual respect and promotes caring.

The downside is that self-assertion involves some degree of risk. Other people may disparage you or feel annoyed by your assertiveness, especially if you have not been very assertive in the past. There are also possible penalties if you assert yourself with a supervisor or boss. The risks may be too high; you can be nicely assertive one day with your boss or supervisor, and the next day you could be out of a job! In this kind of situation, being non-assertive may be the most rational thing to do.

Recognising People who can't take Disapproval

No matter how skilful you may become at expressing healthy disapproval and annoyance, you will find that some people can't take it. Even if you make it clear that you are only criticising the person's behaviour and not the person, they still can't cope with it. What do they do then? They sulk! They sulk because they are experiencing one or more unhealthy negative emotions (such as anger, hurt, self-pity, jealousy and feelings of worthlessness) that spring from unconstructive attitudes.

Another indicator of when it would not be in your best interests to assert yourself is if you work for a boss who is likely to react negatively to such behaviour on your part. You don't want to lose your job, so wisely consider if acting assertively in these circumstances is what you really want — bearing in mind the likely consequences. Before you act assertively with anyone you suspect might not be able to take it, or who might penalize you in some way, take a moment to consider the possible outcome of your assertion. 'Know your customer' is good advice that you would do well to keep in mind in these situations.

Eight Steps to Healthy Self-assertion

We will now briefly outline the eight-step guide to communicating disapproval or annoyance assertively. Remember that assertion is always situation-specific.

Step 1: Get the Person's Attention. This may seem obvious, but one of the errors that people make is to assert themselves when the other person is not attending to what they are saying. If you decide to communicate your feelings at such times, you are liable to be disappointed by the curt response you are likely to get. Stress that it is important to you that you have the opportunity to speak to the other person soon. If the other person puts you off more than twice, you may well have to insist that he or she listens to you. However, if the other person is reasonable, then a polite request to be listened to with their full attention, will usually have the desired effect. For example, in the following vignette, Tracy begins by saying: 'Joe, I want to discuss something important with you, and I need your full attention. Is this a good time?'

Finally, when you do get the other person's attention, make sure that you keep it. Ensure that both of you are not disturbed. Choose a private place where you can't be overheard or disturbed.

Setp 2: Describe Objectively the Other Person's Behaviour that you have Difficulty with. When you bring to the attention of the other person the behaviour that you don't like, it is important that you do so as

128

objectively as possible. Don't give your own interpretations of the facts or motives or intentions. Stick to the facts! In her confrontation with Joe, Tracy stuck to the facts. This is what she said, 'OK. Straight after I gave you the present I had bought you, the phone rang and you spent twenty minutes talking to Tom.'

If Tracy had only communicated her *interpretation* of Joe's behaviour, chances are that an argument would have followed. Suppose Tracy had said something like, 'OK. Straight after I gave you the present, you showed a lack of appreciation of me.'

Joe would probably have gone on the defensive, because he would feel he was being accused of lack of appreciation; that it was not a fact and that he knew it. If you compare these two statements you will see that the first objectively based statement communicates precisely what behaviour Tracy is objecting to. The second interpretation-based statement conveys a judgement on the motive or intention that may not be correct. This may lead to a type of exchange heard frequently in homes namely, 'What did I do?' 'You know what you did.'

Step 3: Communicate your Healthy Negative Feelings. This is important for several reasons. First, it enables you to make your presence felt with the other person. You communicate your feelings that there is something wrong in the relationship and that you want to put it right. It is important at this stage to express your feelings honestly, without evasion, without attacking the other person, and without trying to justify yourself in a defensive manner. Secondly, you get your feelings off your chest. Thirdly, expressing your healthy negative emotions is an antidote to the powerlessness you may experience when you sulk over unfair or inconsiderate treatment. Finally, always remember communicating your healthy negative feelings to the other person promotes intimacy and closeness.

Tracy did just that: 'I feel annoyed and disappointed that you did this.' A mistake people sometimes make is to blame their feelings on the other person. When you shift the burden of responsibility for your feelings on to the other person, and this will frequently lead to an aggressive or defensive response from that person. So use 'I feel' language rather than 'You made me feel' language.

Step 4: Check your Interpretations and Invite a Response. Here it is important to state that your interpretation is not a fact. If you state it as fact, this puts the other person on the defensive, even though your interpretation may be correct. Frame your interpretation as a possibility to be explored rather than a fact that cannot be denied. Finally, invite a response from the other person with respect to your interpretation in order to encourage a dialogue on the issue. Tracy's response was, 'and I want to check out with you whether or not you appreciate me. Let's start with that issue.' That is likely to be more encouraging to Joe than the definite 'and you don't appreciate me'.

Step 5: Listen to the Other's Response and Give Feedback. Listen carefully to the other person's response. If you are genuine in holding your interpretation as a possible explanation of the other person's behaviour rather than a factual explanation, then you will be able to listen to what the other person has to say with an open mind. If you listen with an open mind you will be able to evaluate the other person's response against your own alternative explanation, and what you objectively know about the person before giving feedback.

In Tracy's case, Joe replied to her accusation with an explanation of his behaviour that focused on his difficulty in ending telephone conversations with his friends. This tallied with one of Tracy's interpretations for Joe's behaviour and fitted with what she objectively knew about him. She was genuinely pleased to learn that he did appreciate her, and decided to tell him so.

However, if Tracy did not believe Joe's response, what could she have done? She should still give feedback, but in a way that communicated her scepticism about his explanation without putting him down. For example: 'Joe, I find it difficult to accept that. I wonder if you are being honest with yourself and with me. I'm not putting you down, nor will I if it's true that you took me for granted. Why not think about it again?'

Note how important it is to express your feelings in a way that respects the other person rather than putting them down.

Step 6: State your Preferences Clearly and Specifically.
The next step is to state clearly what you want from the other person. It is important to do this in concrete terms, otherwise the other person will not know specifically what you are asking him or her to do, or not do. Remember also not to escalate your desires into demands. Remind yourself that while it is healthy to desire, there is no law of the universe that you have to get what you want, no matter how important it is to you.

Step 7: Request Agreement from the Other Person. After you have respectfully expressed your preference for some kind of behavioural change from the other person, it is important for you to ask the person whether or not they are prepared to make that change. If they say yes, then you can go on to discuss how they might do this, and what role, if any, you might play in helping them change. If they say no, then you can ask them what changes, if any, they are prepared to make. If they refuse to make any changes, then you may have to re-evaluate your relationship with that person.

Step 8: Communicate any Relevant Information Concerning Future Episodes. The final step involves you communicating any information that you want the other person to have, relevant to any similar future episodes. Thus Tracy said: 'The next time this happens, I'll mention my feelings to you at the time.'

In addition to communicating your intentions about what you will do the next time the other person behaves in the same way, you can ask him or her how he or she would like you to respond. Thus Tracy could have asked: 'The next time this happens, how would you like me to bring this to your attention?'

Finally, you could ask the other person what he or she will do differently in future, when faced with a similar situation. For example, Tracy could say: 'The next time one of your friends phones at an inappropriate time, what are you going to do differently?'

Negotiating Disagreements and Balancing Mutual Rights

The heading of this section covers a wide field of growing importance at every level in society, ranging from negotiations between friends, lovers, and partners, through to management — labour disputes, through to international top-level meetings between nuclear arms negotiators. As Roger Fisher and William Ury point out in their highly acclaimed book *Getting to Yes: Negotiating Agreement Without Giving In* (Houghton Mifflin), everyone negotiates. In this section we can do no more than scratch the surface of this important subject, but the groundwork for getting to grips with some basic insights has already been done in Chapter 3 and of course, in the present chapter. Since our purpose in writing this book is to help you to cope with life when the going gets tough, and to surmount the psychological or emotional problems that often get in the way of a successful resolution of practical matters, we shall concentrate on these psychological aspects rather than the technical details of negotiating strategy.

The Importance of Perception. How you see the world depends to a large extent on your own perspective and the position you are in. Thus understanding the other person's thinking is not just a useful approach to resolving your problem. As Fisher and Ury remark, 'Their thinking *is* the problem.' Reality as each of us sees, it constitutes the heart of the negotiation problem. The ability to see ourselves and the situation as the other person sees it, is one of the most valuable skills you can acquire if you want to understand and influence the other person. Conveying empathic understanding, means understanding the power of the other person's point of view — and the emotional force with which they believe in it. To accomplish this you have to be prepared to withhold judgement while you try to see and feel things from their point of view.

133

Understanding the other's point of view doesn't mean agreeing with it. However, clearer understanding of the other's point of view may enable you to get a better understanding of the merits of that point of view, and that is a bonus, because it can reduce the area of conflict and advance your more enlightened self-interest.

Watch your Interpretations! If you have a biased perception of someone you may find it difficult to avoid putting the worst possible interpretation on what the other person says or does. The cost of these interpretations is that you tend to neglect openings leading to agreement, and subtle changes in the other person's negotiating position are ignored.

Don't blame! You should be fairly well aware by now of the pernicious effects of blame. In blame, we denigrate and condemn the person for his misdeeds or failures, instead of objectively looking at the problem and trying to work out a feasible solution. Blaming someone is usually counter-productive, in that the person will become defensive and resist what you have to say. The motto 'don't entangle the person with the problem' is excellent device, and will help you to focus on the problem rather than the person behind the problem.

Emotions: Yours and theirs. Emotions are an essential part of our humanity. However, there are two kinds of emotions: healthy emotions and unhealthy emotions. The unhealthy negative emotions, such as anger, are the ones that can bedevil negotiations and often bring them to a sudden end. It is often more important to deal initially with emotions such as anger, anxiety, or worry in a bitter dispute than simply talking, for until such emotions are dealt with, and replaced by healthier emotions, the talking is likely to get bogged down in mutual recrimination.

Allow people present to express their feelings and get them off their chests. Explain that holding on to unhealthy negative feelings will almost always be counter-productive and, by sharing that knowledge with the other person or the other side, try to eliminate these negative feelings and replace them with more helpful rational alternatives.

Improve your Communication! Communication is the life blood of negotiation. The better the communication, the better in general the negotiation is likely to be. Unfortunately, good communication is not easy — it's a skill we have to learn. Here are some useful points to keep in mind:

- Whatever you say, it is almost certain that the other person will hear something different from what you meant to convey. This is because differing perceptions will filter out some of what you say, while other aspects of your utterances may be accorded undue significance.

- Even if you are talking clearly and directly, the other person may not hear you. The words may be heard, but the meaning will be missed because listening is an active process. Or the other person may be so busy figuring out what to say in response to your previous utterances, that he considered so important, that he forgot to pay attention to what followed next.

- Then there is the problem of misunderstanding. You and they may be using the same words, but do the same words mean the same thing to each of you? This is where active listening plays so important a part. Active listening consists of paraphrasing back to the speaker what you understood him or her to say: 'Did I understand correctly that you are saying that ...?' The advantage is that the other person will have the satisfaction of being heard and understood.

- Good listening means paying close attention to what is said, asking the other party to spell out carefully and clearly what they mean, and to request that ideas and proposals be repeated if there is any ambiguity or uncertainty. While you are listening, make a real effort to understand others as they see themselves.

- If you have established a basis for mutual trust, fine. Without trust, not much of any kind of a relationship can be established. However, even if you are still in the process of building trust between you, try to structure the negotiation as a joint enterprise, a side-by-side activity in which both you and the other party, with your differing interests and perceptions, are trying to accomplish a common task.

- Separate the people from the problem; view people as fallible human beings and deal with the problem on its merits. Focus on your mutual interests, rather than striving to uphold positions.

These, are just a few pointers to the task of acquiring good negotiating skills. Keep practising them, and you may be surprised at the results you will achieve.

SIX

How to Keep Coping When the Going Remains Tough

*I*deally, we hope to help you develop a philosophy and approach to living that can increase your effectiveness and happiness in *all* areas of life — at work, at play, in parenting, in living successfully with others, and in enhancing your own health and personal welfare.

9 In this final chapter we are going to show you how to maintain the gains you have made so far. We shall assume that you have made progress in changing some of your self-defeating thoughts and behaviours, and are feeling more confident of coping with life.

You will recall that in chapter 1 we stated that our purpose in writing this book was to equip you with a sound understanding of the basic principles of REBT, together with an effective method of applying them to typical problems that you may encounter when the going gets tough. In this context, you can think of REBT as 'Rational Effectiveness Behaviour Training', for that's what it is: training to develop the psychological 'muscle' you need, to cope with various negative life experiences, rather than being overwhelmed by them when life presents you with difficult choices.

So far, so good. There will be times, though, when you are likely to fall back into old habits of thinking and behaving because that's human nature. Nobody is perfect, and practically all of us take one step backward for every two or three steps we move forward.

One Step Back, Two Steps Ahead! or How to Control Messing up Even Occasionally

There is a basic reason why people fall back, even when they have worked hard at acquiring a more rational outlook. We have evidence that we humans are born to think irrationally, although we are also born with the capability of thinking rationally — otherwise we would not have survived! We seem to act self-defeatingly on numerous occasions because we find it easier to be short-term hedonists, who would rather go for the pleasure or ease of the moment. This is because we do what we 'feel' like doing at the time, instead of taking some other action that is less appealing — but that our common sense tells us would be more in our long-term interests. That is why some of us over-indulge in alcohol, or food, or go on some other kind of binge that we usually end up regretting.

So what can we do about it, this unfortunate habit we humans have of repeatedly messing things up when we do actually achieve a measure of progress?

Accept Yourself as a Fallible Human! This means accepting yourself as someone who from time to time will make mistakes, *and* refusing to put yourself down for making these mistakes. It's easy to fall into the trap of condemning yourself as a stupid or worthless person when you find yourself getting angry with someone, or when you feel anxious about an important interview. For example, one day Lynn lost her temper with her solicitor boss when asked to give up her evening, in order to work late typing a submission urgently required in court the following morning. Lynn felt depressed over having lost her temper because she believed, 'I absolutely must not become angry. I should be able to keep my cool. 'This shows what an idiot I am; I'll *never* learn to control my temper!'

Or take the case of Tom, who became extremely anxious the night before an important interview for a supervisory appointment. 'Here I am panicking over this interview I'm going to tomorrow. I thought I'd learned to deal with anxiety. What a hopeless person I am! I'll *never* learn how to conquer my anxiety!'

If you verbally flagellate yourself when you fall back into old irrational thinking patterns and self-defeating habits you thought you had eliminated — or at least controlled — you make it much more difficult to see exactly why you slipped back. So long as you feel bad, ashamed or angry for having acted inappropriately or self-defeatingly, you give yourself a problem about a problem. You now have a double problem to tackle instead of just the original problem. So, what do you tackle first, the primary problem that has re-presented itself, or the secondary problem of castigating and rating yourself as a weak or stupid person?

Give up Your Self-rating! Use the highly important REBT principle of refusing to rate *you*, your *self*. Evaluate only your acts, deeds, and traits. Remind yourself that you are only a person who acts well or badly, but never a good person or a bad person.

If you commit to memory the words of advice in the previous paragraph and convince yourself that they make sense, then you will see your backsliding as normal. You will see it as something that happens to almost all people from time to time. You will see it as part of human fallibility, and not feel ashamed or weak or stupid. You are just a normal human being who

141

occasionally acts badly or inappropriately, but who can learn to turn these lapses to advantage and behave less ineffectually in the future.

Go Back to your A-B-Cs!

When you backslide, accept your backsliding as normal — that's the first step. If you are feeling ashamed because some old symptoms have returned, tackle your shame, your self-denigration, before you do anything else.

Begin by reminding yourself of what you once did to bring about an improvement. Focus exactly on those thoughts, feelings, and behaviours you changed in the past, and pinpoint the iBs you identified then as the cause of your troubled emotions and behaviour, and go over what you did to challenge and dispute those iBs. Don't be dismayed to find that iBs you had previously Disputed and dismissed have now returned! Almost any emotional problem can be shown to consist of one or more of the three Major Irrational Beliefs and their variants.

These three core iBs and their variants lie at the root of virtually all emotional problems and self-defeating behaviours.

Can you see now how easy it might be for these old iBs to slip back and cause some of your problems to return? Ask yourself, 'Are long-standing habits easily changed?' For example, is it 'easy' to go on a diet and stick to it? Haven't you heard of some friend or acquaintance who seemed to have given up an old habit like smoking, only to go back to it again? And again! Giving up an undesirable habit requires *persistent* hard work.

The A-B-C Model of Emotional Disturbance. Begin by clearly seeing for yourself what you did to bring on your old symptoms.

Thus, at **A** (*Activating Event*), let's say you have experienced some negative, or potentially negative, event — such as rejection or failure. Let's take the example of Lynn, who is condemning herself for having lost her temper with her boss. In this case, **A** stands for Lynn's outburst of anger.

At **C** (emotional and behavioural *Consequences*), Lynn is feeling worthless because she allowed herself to become angry, a personal failure she regards as totally unacceptable.

At **B** (*Belief System*), Lynn is telling herself something about what happened at **A**. Since she is upset, she is clearly telling herself something to create her upset feeling. How do we know that? Do you recall REBT Insight No. 1, which we introduced in Chapter 1, page 12?

It follows that if you want to rid yourself of disturbed feelings, you need to rid yourself of the iBs that lie behind these feelings and replace them with iBs that will lead to healthy feelings and constructive attitudes.

Getting Back to Basics. Unfortunately, it's not as simple as that. Old habitual ways of thinking — your old iBs — don't just roll over and die. You have to keep forcefully and persistently disputing them whenever you see signs that they are creeping back again. So, let's take up at the point where we paused to recall REBT Insight No. 1. You will see that Lynn created her own feeling of worthlessness, with her conclusion that she was no good due to her failure to keep her cool. However,

Lynn also knows she has a choice here; she doesn't *have to* upset herself because she became angry with her boss. Lynn knows that there is a difference between appropriate, healthy, negative feelings (such as sorrow, regret, and annoyance when she acts badly, or fails to achieve her goals) and inappropriate or unhealthy negative feelings (such as depression, anxiety, or self-hatred and self-pity) when she does the wrong thing or fails badly in some endeavour. What is the difference between unhealthy negative feelings and healthy negative feelings? The answer lies in carefully noting the distinguishing features between rBs and iBs. Refer back to Table 1 on page 16, which highlights the features of rationality and irrationality.

When you find yourself slipping back into self-defeating behaviours, look immediately and persistently for the iBs behind them. They are certainly there, and they almost invariably take the form of some dogmatic 'should', 'ought', or 'must'. Let's see how Lynn could go about tackling her despair over losing her temper with her boss. Lynn's beliefs about the episode were:

'I absolutely must not become angry. I should be able to keep my cool after all I've learned about controlling my tendencies to become angry!'

She then concludes:

'This shows what an idiot I am; I'll *never* learn to control my temper!'

Dispute. We suspect that iBs are here from the presence of unqualified demands, and the appearance of the word 'never', which comes under the same absolutist category of unqualified statements.

144

Are Lynn's beliefs logical? It is clear that Lynn strongly wants to avoid getting angry and believes that she should be able to achieve it. However, does it logically follow that because she wants to avoid getting angry that she absolutely must not? Obviously not. There is no logical necessity for Lynn's wishes, or anyone else's, to be granted. By the same token, there is no logical reason to believe that because Lynn took a course designed to help her control her tendencies to become angry, that therefore she should always be in control.

On the basis of her failure to control her temper, Lynn concludes that she'll never learn. It is not difficult to see that this conclusion too is illogical. It doesn't follow that because Lynn failed to keep her temper on this occasion that she can *never* keep it. This conclusion is another example of gross exaggeration.

Are Lynn's beliefs realistic? Well, if you believe that you absolutely must not get angry then your belief implies that there is some law of the universe that your wishes absolutely must prevail. Is that consistent with reality? Clearly it isn't.

Do Lynn's beliefs help her achieve her goals? Until she gives up her perfectionistic demand that she must never be angry and stops hating herself for failing to live up to her unrealistic expectation, Lynn is likely to remain fearful of losing control of her anger and to become self-hating whenever she does so.

Lynn's rational alternative approach. Once Lynn begins to question her various iBs — 'Why must I never get angry? And how does failing at times to control my anger, make me an idiot who can never learn to do better?' — she can answer:

'I very much prefer to control my temper and avoid angry outbursts, but I don't absolutely have to. I certainly don't become worthless because I fail at times to control my angry tendencies, nor does it mean I will never succeed in controlling them. All that these failures mean is that I'm a fallible human being, and that if I work harder in these areas of my life, and possibly other areas, I can lead a less angry and happier life in the future.

Persistent Effort Pays Off. Giving up an undesirable or self-defeating habit requires persistent hard work. Your iBs weren't born yesterday; they have probably been around a long time. At this point, some people might say, 'Quite so, but doesn't that prove that you need to uncover and dig into your past, if you really want to understand and resolve your problems today?' To which, our answer would be:

'Your past history, including events in your early life, as well as your present life conditions, can strongly influence you; but neither your early life nor your present life conditions make you disturbed. Your present philosophy is the main contributor to your current disturbance. Regardless of how or when you acquired your iBs and self-defeating habits in the past, you *now*, in the *present*, choose to believe them — and that is why you are now disturbed.'

These remarks are well summarized by REBT Insight No. 2 on page 147.

If you still feel anxious, depressed, angry, or self-hating more often than you are willing to tolerate, keep looking for those iBs that keep sneaking in. When

REBT Insight No. 1

You feel the way you think, and your thinking, feelings, and behaviour are all interrelated. In effect you largely choose to disturb yourself about the unpleasant negative events (the As) in your life by selecting iBs about your As that lead you to feel angry, anxious, depressed and self-hating. You can also choose rBs that lead you to feel annoyed, sad, or regretful.

REBT Insight No. 2

Regardless of how you disturbed yourself in the past, you are disturbed now because you still believe the iBs which created your disturbed feelings. Moreover, you are still reindoctrinating yourself with these unsustainable beliefs, not because you were previously 'conditioned' to hold these beliefs and now do so 'automatically', but because you are continually reinforcing these ideas by your present inappropriate actions or inaction, in addition to your unrealistic thinking.

REBT Insight No. 3

This is the clear realisation and unflinching acknowledgment that it is your own human tendency to think crookedly that created your emotional problems in the past, and that since these problems have persisted, there is nothing for it but hard work and practice if these are to be uprooted, to the point where they cease to be a problem. That means that repeated rethinking and disputing of iBs together with repeated actions designed to undo them, are necessary if these beliefs are to be extinguished or minimized.

you find them, go after them. Actively and vigorously dispute them and keep doing this over and over again, strongly and persistently. Don't give up too soon! This brings us logically to REBT insight No. 3:

You have now been introduced to the three major Irrational Beliefs and to the three REBT Insights.

The three Major Irrational Beliefs tell you *what* creates emotional and behavioural problems.

The three REBT Insights tell you *how* these three major irrational beliefs and their derivatives create problems, and what you need to do to rid yourself of them. Throughout this book we have focused your attention on Disputing, which is the main method used in REBT to reveal to people the basic irrationalities by which they run a large part of their lives, and that lead to their feelings of disturbance.

However, in addition to Disputing we use several other efficient methods of helping people to surrender their irrationalities. You will recall the message of REBT Insight No. 1: we feel as we think, and we think, feel, and act simultaneously and transactionally. All three modalities — thinking, feeling, and acting — are interrelated and act upon each other. The way we think strongly influences the way we feel and behave. Also, the way we feel and behave feeds back into our thinking.

While you have made a good start at changing your disturbed feelings and self-defeating behaviour by working hard at changing your irrational thinking, you can achieve even better results, by adding to your armour of Disputing techniques several emotive and behavioural methods. Old habits of thinking, feeling, and acting die hard. Recognizing this, we have developed a number of emotive and behavioural techniques to supplement your Disputing techniques, in order to help you deal more efficiently with your emotional problems and to change unhelpful behaviour. We begin with two emotive techniques.

Emotive Ways to Maintain your 'Gains'

Rational Emotive Imagery (REI). This method was originated by Dr Maxie C. Maultsby, Jr. a rational-behavioural psychiatrist, and adapted by Dr Albert Ellis.

To use REI, imagine as vividly as you can, one of the worst possible things that might happen to you that would contribute towards a feeling of anxiety, anger, depression, or worthlessness.

Suppose, for illustration, that you have been to many job interviews and have been rejected time after time. Now imagine you are in your next job-seeking interview and that once more you have been turned down. This is point A (*Activating Event*). Intensely imagine this happening, and that you are feeling very depressed as a result. This is point C (emotional *Consequence*). Try to really get in touch with your feeling of depression. Experience it deeply and acutely, and stay with the feeling for a minute or two.

Now, keeping exactly that same image in mind — being rejected and feeling depressed over losing out yet again — in your imagination make yourself feel *only* sorry or disappointed about what is happening to you. You can do it! Keep working at changing your feeling of depression until you have changed it to mere disappointment, even if only for a few seconds. When you have succeeded in doing so, get in touch with what you told yourself (point **B**) about your rejection to make you feel merely sorry or disappointed rather than depressed.

After managing to change your feeling of depression to a feeling of *only* sorrow or disappointment, you may have told yourself something like, 'It is certainly bad to lose another opportunity and to continue being unemployed, but it doesn't mean that I'll always fail or remain unemployed for ever.

Once you have identified the new thought that you used to change your depressed feeling, see how it is connected with, and creates, your new, more appropriate, feeling of disappointment. Then practice REI for ten to fifteen minutes each day for a minimum of thirty days. Carefully note what your new thinking consisted of. You will probably find that your new thoughts tended to be more factual and realistic, and therefore more rational.

The pay-off is that after a while you will find yourself automatically feeling appropriately sorry or disappointed rather than inappropriately depressed or despairing, not only when you imagine being rejected, but actually when you do get rejected.

Now let's show you another way of building up your 'emotional muscle'.

Shame-attacking Exercises. When people do something wrong in public, behave incompetently, or immorally, they often make themselves feel ashamed. Since shame is a disturbed feeling, you can help to rid yourself of shameful feelings by showing yourself that you create them by insisting that you absolutely must do well. Shame-attacking exercises help you to Dispute and give up these iBs, and to accept yourself with your failings.

First, select some action that you normally would consider risky, foolish, embarrassing, or humiliating. Then do it — *in public!* Don't do anything that would

150

get you into trouble with the law, or cause you to lose your job. Do this 'shameful' act at least once in public so that friends, relatives, or strangers can see you acting 'shamefully'. If you can pick some act that you would like to do but have previously avoided doing because people might think badly of you — for example, expressing disapproval of someone's inconsiderate behaviour in public — so much the better.

The purpose of a shame-attacking exercise is to do something that most people would consider silly or crazy and would scorn or laugh at. But is it 'shameful' or 'embarrassing'? Is it 'humiliating'? No, because the purpose of the exercise is to enable you to convince yourself that nothing is really shameful, embarrassing, or humiliating — unless you *think* it is.

You see, shame and embarrassment don't come from making a social *faux pas* or from acting foolishly in public, but from what you tell yourself about these acts: 'What an idiot I am for letting myself behave like that?' is a typical response to the scorn or derision of others.

However, you have it within your power to say to yourself 'I am doing a stupid thing here, or acting incompetently, but that doesn't make me stupid or incompetent.' And you can go on to tell yourself:

'If others think I am crazy for doing this shame-attacking exercise, that is their prerogative. I can agree with them that I am doing a foolish or socially risky thing, but that doesn't make me a fool as they mistakenly think I am.'

If you persist in thinking along these lines as you do your shame-attacking exercises, you will eventually

151

overcome your feelings of shame and come to realize that nothing is intrinsically shameful or humiliating.

As Eleanor Roosevelt neatly put it, 'Nobody can insult you without your permission.'

We will now move on to consider what behavioural methods you can use to supplement the other methods you have learned to help you overcome you emotional problems.

Behavioural Ways to Maintain your 'Gains'

Homework Assignments: Acting against your iBs. We tend to be habit-forming creatures. We easily acquire and maintain good habits, but we also have the capacity to acquire unhelpful habits such as procrastination, worrying, becoming enraged and so on. Usually, firm resolutions to reform are not enough to make these self-defeating habits disappear. Unless some definite action is taken to eliminate them, bad habits are likely to become entrenched.

We learn by *doing*. The example of desensitization we gave you in the section on shame-attacking exercises, is an effective method of illustrating this point. If you act against your unhelpful habit patterns such as long-held anxieties and phobias, you will improve your chances of eliminating them. Keep risking and doing things you would like to do, but are irrationally afraid of doing — such as socialising, dating or job hunting, etc. Do these things many times, and do them in a 'cold turkey' manner. Once you have succeeded in one of these endeavours and have partly overcome some irrational fear associated with it, keep acting against your irrational fear on a regular basis. Don't give up too soon! Keep working at doing what you are irrationally afraid to do until you are comfortable doing it.

Take sensible risks, but don't take things to foolish extremes. Push yourself to act against your groundless fears and convince yourself that nothing truly terrible will happen when you force yourself to do something you feel uncomfortable about. If you feel uncomfortable when you force yourself to do something you consider 'risky', such as dating an attractive member of the opposite sex, don't cop out! Don't take the 'easy' way out and avoid approaching that person. That way will almost certainly preserve your discomfort for ever! The quickest way to feel comfortable with any activity is to practise doing it until you feel comfortable doing it.

Building Emotional and Intellectual Muscle. Just as you have to exercise to build up physical muscle, so too will you need to practise to build emotional and intellectual muscle. That's what becoming tough-minded really entails: working and practising at finding and Disputing your iBs until your disturbed feelings — be they feelings of anger, anxiety, depression, guilt, or self-hating — have truly disappeared. Then continue doing they same thing many times until your new Rational philosophy becomes hardened and a part of you.

In order for your new philosophy to sink in and become a part of you, it is necessary that you really convince yourself of the following rBs:

- 'I don't need what I want.'
- 'I don't have to get all my wishes fulfilled.'
- 'I can stand being rejected by someone I love — and still lead a happy life.'
- 'People who frustrate me or treat me unfairly are not rotten, damnable individuals.'

- 'No one, especially me, is ever a worthless human being.'
- 'No matter how difficult life conditions may be for me, it isn't horrible or terrible, and I can stand it and still be a reasonably happy individual.'

If you succeed in really convincing yourself of these rBs and precepts, and if you want them to become part of your new philosophy, they almost always will — *if you keep working at it.* And there's the rub!

The trouble is that while many people see the rationality of these ideas and say that they will definitely do them, they frequently *don't* do them! Or they implement or practice them half-heartedly. They intend to do their assignments, but somehow their intentions get mislaid. If you are finding difficulty in carrying out your homework assignments, help is at hand.

Self-management Procedures. Reasons we often hear from people for not doing their homework assignments are:

- 'I'll do it later.'
- 'It's too hard.'
- 'It shouldn't be so hard.'
- 'I have to be in the mood first.'

If you look at these 'reasons' closely, you will see that they are really excuses, and that they stem from Low Frustration Tolerance (LFT). Since you know by now how to dispute the iBs underlying LFT — usually a variant of Major Irrational Belief No. 3 — we will not waste time repeating. Once you effectively dispute the iBs behind your LFT and acquire self-discipline, then you will almost always have an easier time doing your homework assignments.

However, if disputing your LFT iBs fails to move your butt, you can then resort to *operant conditioning*. To use this technique, first select some activity that you particularly enjoy. That might be listening to music, reading, conversing with friends, etc. You then make the performance of your selected activity contingent upon your doing your homework assignment, such as encountering a set number of new acquaintances, giving a public talk, or reading a book. If you fail to carry out the prescribed activity, then no performance of the enjoyable activity!

In cases where that method is not powerful enough to get you going, we use penalizing tasks. These are not intended to damn or punish you. Instead, we give you a stiff penalty, something that you yourself select, that you will promptly incur if you fail to carry out your assignment. These penalties are usually activities you abhor doing, such as eating unpleasant tasting foods, doing boring tasks, cleaning the bathroom and so on. The use of immediate rewards for doing difficult assignments, coupled with the strict and quick enforcement of penalties for not doing them, works very well with many people. If self-monitoring is not working very well for you, you can arrange for supervised monitoring instead. Ask a friend or relative to monitor your performance of the required assignment, and have this person carry out the reinforcement and penalty programme. You will find that if you carry out this programme successfully, you can help yourself with almost any kind of self-discipline problem.

Experience Life to the Full

The emotive and behavioural techniques we introduced in the previous sections are just a few of those that are available to students and practitioners of REBT today. Together with the Disputing methods, you now have the means at your disposal to tackle virtually any emotional problem that may sabotage your ability to enjoy life.

What we have tried to accomplish in this book is to provide you with a set of proven techniques for helping you solve emotional problems by showing you how to uncover the individual set of beliefs — your attributes, expectations, and personal rules of behaviour — that frequently lead to emotional distress. Our ultimate aim, however, is not merely to help you rid yourself of painful emotions and maladaptive behaviours that may be sabotaging your ability to live a happier life. Ideally, we hope to help you develop a philosophy and approach to living that can increase your effectiveness and happiness in *all* areas of life — at work, at play, in parenting, in living successfully with others, and in enhancing your own health and personal welfare.

Becoming your own Teacher. If you have followed us so far, you should be able to explain in your own words how emotional disturbances usually arise, how they become ingrained habits, and what can be done to eliminate them. Also, if you presently have an emotional problem, we would expect you to realize that the ways in which you bring it about are not unique, and that practically all emotional and behavioural difficulties spring from, and are sustained by, the same source — namely, iBs.

Moreover, regardless of what form your disturbed emotions and behaviour take, you can overcome them by persistently Disputing and acting against the iBs by using the techniques outlined and demonstrated throughout this book. By taking responsibility for your own emotional and behavioural difficulties instead of attributing them to your upbringing, or your heredity, or the society you live in, you become, in effect, your own REBT teacher.

If you know how to rid yourself of one particular problem, then there is no reason why you cannot generalize from working on that particular problem or working on any other problem. If you work hard and persistently at using the REBT principles and techniques you've been learning to date, you can get to the point where you rarely upset yourself about anything.

Some Final Reminders

In this final section we focus on a number of key ideas that you have already covered, but that are essential to keep in mind if you wish to cope effectively with the stresses and strains of life with minimal disturbance to your emotional equilibrium.

- Acquire rational self acceptance. Accept yourself as being valuable to yourself just because you exist, because you are alive, and have some capacity to enjoy yourself. Refuse to measure your intrinsic worth, by your extrinsic accomplishments or by socially fashionable criteria of success such as popularity, achievement, material possessions, service to others, devotion to God and so on. Strive actively to accomplish what you set your heart on, but to enjoy yourself rather than aiming to prove yourself.

- Try to see clearly the difference between appropriate or healthy negative feelings — such as sadness, sorrow, regret, concern, and annoyance —

when the going is tough and your important desires and goals are frustrated, and inappropriate or unhealthy feelings — such as depression, self-pity, shame, embarrassment, self-hatred, anxiety, and hostility or rage.

- Remind yourself of the three REBT Insights, particularly No. 3! There is no other way for you to overcome longstanding or deep-seated emotional problems, but by continually questioning and challenging your iBs, and by working at changing these.

- Memorize the three Major Irrational Beliefs, and look out for their variants and derivatives. Repeatedly show yourself that it is difficult to become and remain, emotionally disturbed in any way at all if you throw out your absolutistic, dogmatic shoulds, oughts, and musts, and consistently replace them with flexible desires and preferences.

- Learn to view life as a process of continual growth, and establish priorities and life goals. Be adventurous, not a stick-in-the-mud. Life is for living. Monitor your progress towards your goals. Revise them when that seems desirable, and keep goal oriented for the rest of your life. But remember, although it is highly desirable to achieve your goals and realize your dreams, it is never an absolute necessity!

- Review you relationships with others. Try to cultivate better relations with those you love or with those who are important to you by communicating an understanding of their feelings and of what 'makes them tick'. If other relationships

158

were once meaningful or important to you but are now no longer so and may continue to drain your time or clutter up your life, terminate them without anger or guilt.

- Overcome barriers to living more productively and enjoyably. Avoid that great thief of time, love, and money: procrastination. Self-defeating procrastination is the result of Low Frustration Tolerance (LFT). Don't let the blight of procrastination establish itself in your life! Combat it vigorously and persistently each and every time you find it trying to sneak in and entwine you with ideas such as, 'I have to feel comfortable before tackling important tasks', or 'I have to be in the mood to do them'. At that rate, you might never do them?

  If you find it difficult to get going, use the self-management procedures we described in previous sections to get you started. Wasting time is really wasting life, and you are in sole charge of your own direction in life. Since this life is the only one you know for sure you have, why not make the most of it?

- And finally, we offer you one of REBT's favourite maxims that was first expressed by Reinhold Niebuhr: 'Grant me the courage to change the things I can change, the serenity to accept those I cannot change, and the wisdom to know the difference.'

□□□

Secrets of Success

Charles Newton

When was the last time you tried to punch a hole in the sky?

Tests Pilots, punching into stratosphere, climbing to undreamt heights in jets and rocket planes, have a phrase they use to describe their work.

They call it 'punching holes in the sky.'

That is what we are meant to do with our lives, to climb beyond the humdrum, to reach beyond the preoccupation of daily existence. However, more often that not, when it comes to living, we settle for the mediocre. The sky is too high to think of. It is the impossible that stops us. But nonetheless it is the challenge of the impossible that gets life out of its rut and onto a highway that leads us to our goal.

Think big, work hard and have the courage to dream.

Remember, if you don't care for your dreams, who will.

Whatever your personal goals, this book will help you become the person you have always wanted to be.

pp 144 | Rs. 60.00

Available at all bookshops or by V.P.P.

Orient Paperbacks
Madarsa Road, Kashmere Gate, Delhi-110 006